THE

GLENS OF

RANNOCH

THE GLENS OF RANNOCH

A personal survey of the Glens of Rannoch
for mountainbikers and walkers

by

Peter D. Koch-Osborne

CICERONE PRESS
MILNTHORPE, CUMBRIA

© P.D. Koch - Osborne 1994
ISBN 1 85284 170 2
Reprinted 2004

British Library Cataloguing-in-Publication Data.
A catalogue record for this book is
available from the British Library

What would the world be, once bereft
Of wet and wilderness? Let them be left,
O let them be left, wilderness and wet;
Long live the weeds and the wilderness yet.

Gerard Manley Hopkins
Inversnaid.

Cover pictures :- Loch Ossian Youth Hostel
Black Corries

Introduction

Access to the tracks and paths on the following pages can never be regarded as an absolute right by the cyclist or walker. All land is privately owned and it is only the good nature of the landowner that allows us to travel unhindered over his land. In law no such term as trespass exists in Scotland, nuisance or damage has to be proven in order to eject persons from the land but in practice sensible conduct is all that is required to maintain free access. Respect the grouse shooting and deer stalking seasons whatever your views on the subject of 'blood sports'. The author has not once met with any animosity in meetings with estate workers. Your good conduct will keep it this way.

Conservation of the wild areas of Scotland is of paramount importance. Much has been written elsewhere but users of this guide must appreciate that the very ground over which you walk or cycle will be damaged if care is not taken. Please don't use a bike on soft peat paths and tread carefully on other than a stony track. Many of the tracks are in themselves an eyesore and any "development" can cause irreparable damage. Make sure, as walkers and cyclists, we encourage the conservation of our wilderness areas without the pressure of our activities causing further damage. In publishing this book a great deal of trust is placed upon you, the reader, to respect the needs of the region. If all you need is exercise - go to a sports centre! but if you appreciate the unique qualities of the wild places they are yours to enjoy..... carefully! Careless conduct not only damages what we seek to enjoy but, equally seriously, gives landowners good reason to restrict access.

<u>The Maps</u> on the following pages give sufficient detail for exploration of the glens but the Ordnance Survey Landranger maps of the region should also be used if the full geographical context of the area is to be fully appreciated. These maps and the knowledge of their proper use are essential if a long tour or cross country route is to be undertaken.

<u>The mountain bike</u>, or ATB-all terrain bike, has in the author's opinion been badly named. It does not belong on the high tops but is ideal in the glens covering at least twice the distance of the average walker, quietly, whilst still allowing a full appreciation of the surroundings and providing further exploration into the wilderness especially on short winter days. The bike must be a well maintained machine complete with a few essential spares as a broken bike miles from anywhere can be serious. Spare gear is best carried in strong panniers on good carriers. Poor quality bikes and accessories simply will not last. Front panniers help distribute weight and prevent "wheelies". Mudguards are essential. Heavy rucksacks are tiring and put more weight onto one's already battered posterior! The brightly coloured "high profile" image of mountainbiking is unsuited to the remote glens. These wild areas are sacred and need treating as such.

<u>Clothing</u> for the mountainbiker is an important consideration, traditional road cycling gear is un-suitable. High ankle trainers are best for summer, and light weight walking boots for winter cycling. A zipped fleece jacket with waterproof top and overtrousers with spare thin sweatshirts etc

should be included for easily adjusting temperature. The wearing of a helmet is a personal choice, it depends how you ride, where you ride and the value you place on your head! In any event a thin balaclava will be required under a helmet in winter or a thick one in place of a helmet. Good waterproof gloves are essential. Fingers and ears get painfully cold on a long descent at −5°C. Protection against exposure should be as for mountain walking. Many of the glens are as high as English hilltops. The road cyclists shorts or longs will keep legs warm in summer only. In winter walkers breeches and overtrousers are more suitable.

Clothing for the walker has had much written about it elsewhere. Obviously full waterproofs, spare warm clothing, spare food etc. should be included. In winter conditions the longer through routes should never be attempted alone or by the inexperienced.

Mountainbikers and walkers alike should never be without a good map, this book (!), a whistle (and knowledge of its proper use), compass, emergency rations, and in winter a sleeping bag and cooker may be included even if an overnight stop is not planned. Word of your planned route should be left together with your estimated time of arrival. The bothies must be left tidy with firewood for the next visitor. Don't be too proud to remove someone else's litter. Join the Mountain Bothies Association to help support the maintenance of these simple shelters. It should not be necessary to repeat the Country Code and the Mountain Bike Code, the true lover of the wild places needs peace and space - not rules and regulations.

River crossings are a major consideration when planning long or "through" routes virtually anywhere in Scotland. It must be remembered that snowmelt from the high mountains can turn what is a fordable stream in early morning into a raging torrent by mid afternoon. Walkers should hold on to each other, in three's, forming a triangle if possible. Rivers can be easier to cross with a bike, as the bike can be moved, brakes applied, lean't on then the feet can be re-positioned and so on. The procedure is to remove boots and socks, replace boots, make sure you can't drop anything and cross - ouch! Drain boots well, dry your feet and hopefully your still dry socks will help to warm your feet up. Snowmelt is so cold it hurts. Choose a wide shallow point to cross and above all don't take risks.

Ascents on a bike should be tackled steadily in a very low gear and sitting down wherever possible. While front panniers prevent "wheelies" sitting down helps the rear wheel grip. Standing on the pedals causes wheel slip, erosion, and is tiring. Pushing a laden mountainbike is no fun and usually the result of tackling the lower half of a climb standing up, in the wrong gear or too fast.

Descents on a bike can be exhilarating but a fast descent is hard on the bike, the rider, and erodes the track if wheels are locked. It is also ill-mannered towards others who may be just around the next bend.

Last but not least other users of the tracks need treating with respect - it may be the owner! Bad conduct can only lead to restricted access, spoiling it for us all.

The Maps 1

The maps are drawn to depict the most important features to the explorer of the glens. North is always at the top of each map and all maps, apart from the detail sketches, are to the same scale :- 1km or 0·6 miles being shown on each map. An attempt has been made to present the maps in a pictorially interesting way. A brief explanation of the various features is set out below :-

<u>Tracks</u>:- One of the prime objects of this book is to grade the tracks according to "roughness". This information is essential to the mountainbiker and useful to the walker. With due respect to the Ordnance Survey one "other road, drive or track" can take twice as long to cycle along as another yet both may be depicted in the same way. The authors attempt at grading is set out below:-

metalled road, not too many fortunately, public roads are generally included only to locate the start of a route.

good track, hardly rutted, nearly as fast as a road to cycle on but can be boring to walk far on. Most are forest tracks.

the usual rutted "Landrover" track, rough but all easily rideable on a mountainbike, not too tedious to walk on.

rough, very rutted track nearly all rideable, can be very rough even for walking. Either very stony or overgrown or boggy.

walker's path, usually over 50% is rideable and included especially as a part of a through route. Details given on each map.

<u>Relief</u> is depicted in two ways. The heavy black lines are now a commonly used method of depicting main mountain summits, ridges and spurs thus:-

Contour lines are also used, at 50m intervals up to about 600m. This adds "shape" to the glens as mapped and gives the reader an idea of how much climbing is involved. Reference to the gradient profiles at the start of each section compares the various routes:-

_500 m_   _550 m_   _600 m_

<u>Crags</u> in the high mountains are shown thus:-

....with major areas of scree shown dotted

<u>Rivers</u> generally "uncrossable" are shown as two lines whilst streams, generally "crossable" are shown using a single line. Note:- great care is needed crossing even the larger streams. Falling in can cause embarrassment at best, exposure or drowning at worst. Please don't take risks - besides you'd get this book wet !!

loch or lochan

<u>Buildings</u> and significant ruins are shown as a:-■

<u>Bridges</u> are rather obviously shown thus:-
There are so many trees I wish there were an easier way of drawing them -but there isn't! I'm fed up with drawing trees!!

etc etc.....

11

Rannoch Glens - West

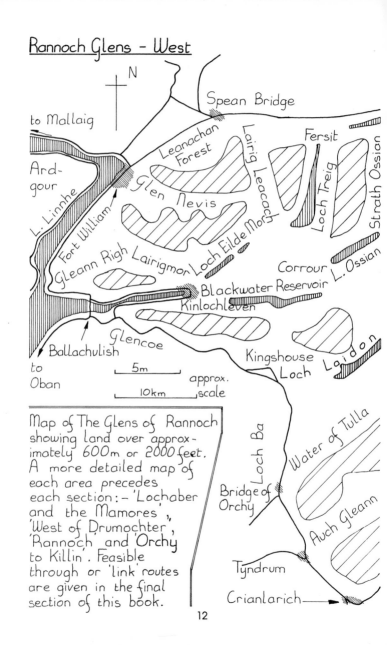

N

to Mallaig

Spean Bridge

Fersit

Strath Ossian

Leanachan Forest

Lairig Leacach

Loch Treig

Ard-gour

L. Linnhe

Glen Nevis

Fort William

Loch Eilde Mor

Corrour

L. Ossian

Gleann Righ Lairigmor

Blackwater Reservoir

Kinlochleven

Ballachulish

Glencoe

Kingshouse Loch

Loch Laidon

to Oban

5m

10km

approx. scale

Map of The Glens of Rannoch showing land over approx-imately 600m or 2000 feet. A more detailed map of each area precedes each section:- 'Lochaber and the Mamores', 'West of Drumochter', 'Rannoch' and 'Orchy to Killin'. Feasible through or 'link' routes are given in the final section of this book.

Loch Ba

Water of Tulla

Bridge of Orchy

Auch Gleann

Tyndrum

Crianlarich

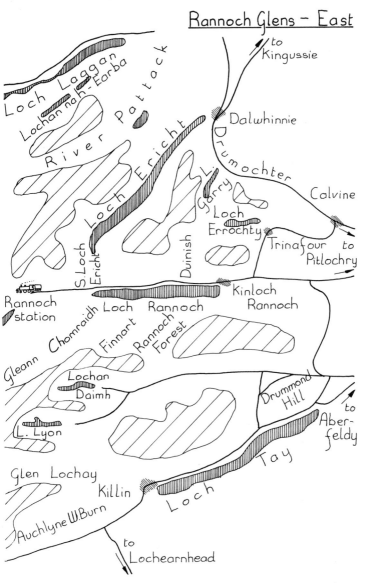

Lochaber and the Mamores

Lochaber and the Mamores

Access:- The main A82 road to Fort William via the Ballachulish bridge transports many thousands of visitors to this area every year. The uninspiring village of Kinlochleven is usually by-passed, however despite it's first impressions, don't miss out the good routes in this area. The road continues via Spean Br. giving access to the forests north of "The Ben." Great advantage can be taken of rail facilities in the area and a close study of the timetables allows one-way sorties to and from the central region of Rannoch Moor - without spending nights out in the wild.

Accommodation:- Fort William provides everything- usually in excess, peace and quiet it does not provide! The wide range of accommodation, backed up by the Tourist Information service is however useful as a springboard to the real attractions in the high glens, moor and mountains. Kinlochleven has improved of late due to the West Highland Way pouring walkers into the area and various establishments are now available. Campsites in the area vary from very basic to the Bunree Caravan Club site (no tents). Prices seem high almost irrespective of facilities, such is the demand.

Geographical Features:- The high mountains give way to moors as one travels east. Rannoch Moor is not flat as often imagined, so there is an abundance of dramatic, scenic interest in the area. Rainfall is a well known 'feature', visit in May or June if you can to avoid the worst - and also avoid the midges!

Mountains:- Ben Nevis, the Aonachs, Grey Corries, Mamores and Aonach Eagach - arguably the finest mountain region in mainland Britain. The routes given allow access via the 'back door' to the mountains from the remote side, unseen by the tourist. Ben Nevis looks its finest from the central Moor, standing high and majestic with lesser mountains below and before it. These routes are the purist's way to the heights.

16

Rivers:- The experienced map-reader will assess the size of rivers not only upon the weather conditions but by a glance at the area the river drains. Such use of maps in this region will soon reveal the rivers are twice the normal size; it is often not possible to cross safely within only 3 or 4 miles of a river's source. It is essential therefore to study the location of bridges and any likely crossing points before setting out. The area from the Nevis gorge to Corrour needs careful study to avoid an unwelcome soaking or a *long* walk!

Forests:- Leanachan Forest, bicycle friendly thanks to the Forestry Commission, provides a varied if tame area for short walks or family bike rides. An ideal starting ground for mountainbiking. The Nevis Forest provides an alternative to the metalled road. The only other significant wooded area is the natural deciduous woodland above Kinlochleven - a change from conifers!

Lochs:- Blackwater Reservoir lies uncomfortably across the Moor, looking like the bleak stretch of flooded moorland it is. Little Loch Eilde Mor and its neighbour Loch Eilde Beag look more at home - despite having a dam. Loch Treig reservoir lies in a dramatic pathless glen, probably best appreciated from the window of the train - but that's cheating.

Emergency:- All routes run out to a public road with phone box and/or houses. The end of the public road in Glen Nevis can be deserted on a bad day and there is no shelter. The weather can change in hours and again referring to the Nevis gorge-Corrour area you are very much on your own and it is a long way to just about anywhere. Leave word of your route, estimated time of arrival, watch the weather and don't travel alone. This is a serious area in winter. If in doubt call off or modify your intended route. People have died doggedly sticking to their plans whatever the weather. No apologies for driving these points home. It has to be said. We'll now proceed carefully into the area and enjoy its rain soaked delights!

Lochaber and the Mamores Routes 1

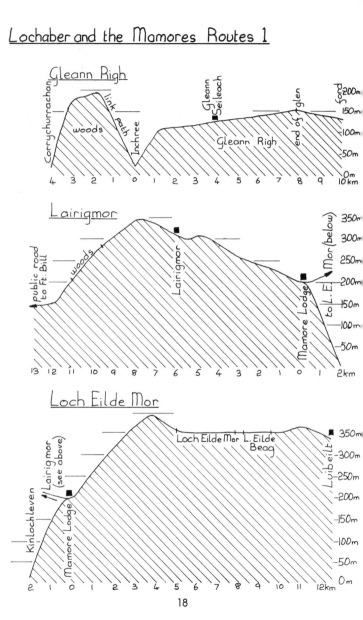

Gleann Righ

Corrychurrachan · woods · link path · Inchree · Gleann Seileach · Gleann Righ · end of glen · ford

200m · 150m · 100m · 50m · 0m

4 3 2 1 0 1 2 3 4 5 6 7 8 9 10 km

Lairigmor

public road to Ft. Bill · woods · Lairigmor · Mamore Lodge · to L. E. Mor (below)

350m · 300m · 250m · 200m · 150m · 100m · 50m · 2km

13 12 11 10 9 8 7 6 5 4 3 2 1 0 1

Loch Eilde Mor

Kinlochleven · Mamore Lodge · Lairigmor (see above) · Loch Eilde Mor · L. Eilde Beag · Luibeilt

350m · 300m · 250m · 200m · 150m · 100m · 50m · 0m

2 1 0 1 2 3 4 5 6 7 8 9 10 11 12km

Lochaber and the Mamores Routes 2

Blackwater Reservoir

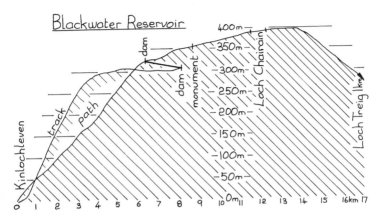

Glen Nevis

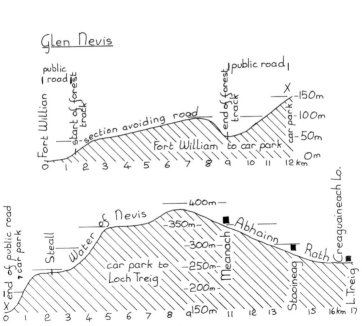

19

Lochaber and the Mamores Routes 3

Leanachan Forest

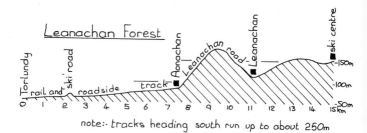

note:- tracks heading south run up to about 250m

Lairig Leacach

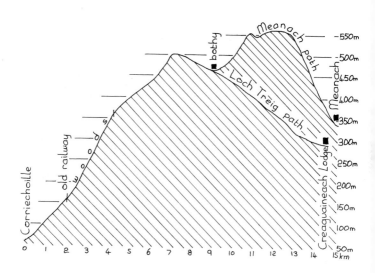

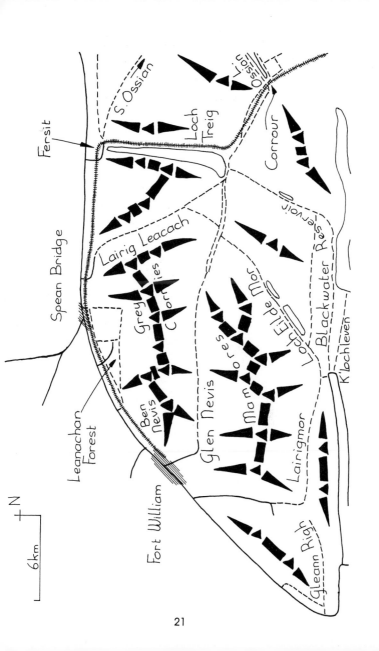

N

6km

Spean Bridge

Fort William

Leanachan Forest

Ben Nevis

Glen Nevis

Lairig Leacach

Grey Corries

Mamores

Loch Eilde Mor

Lairigmor

Gleann Righ

Kinlochleven

Blackwater Res

Corrour

Loch Treig

Fersit

Loch Ossian

S. Ossian

Gleann Righ 1

Access to Gleann Righ is either from the A82 at Inchree or from the car park/picnic area at Corrychurrachan. The busy A82 is to be avoided by cyclists although there is a pavement much of the way. Note the link path joining the woods to Gleann Righ. Also note carefully the different grades of path and track.

Fort William

397m

575m

Loch Linnhe

views

conc. bridge

old quarry

seat

better down than 'up'-on a bike!!

206m

seat

S.P.

To Waterfalls

gate and cattle grid

Gleann Seileach

150m

200m

250m

Opposite

Continued

car park

Inchree

gate

Coran Narrows

A82

Righ

Gleann

Falls

-magnificent!

Abhainn Righ

150m

200m

250m

387m

waterfalls walk not a bike ride.

Bunree Caravan Club site

A82

Onich

50m

100m

150m

200m

N

1km

Ballachulish

22

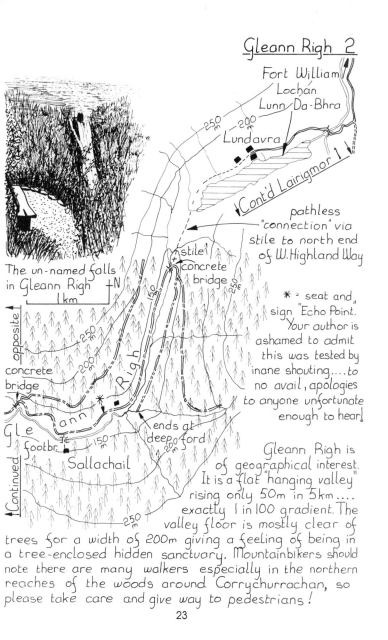

Fort William

Lochán Lunn Da-Bhra

250 m 200

Lundavra

Cont'd Lairigmor 1

pathless "connection" via stile to north end of W. Highland Way

stile

concrete bridge

250 m

The un-named falls in Gleann Righ

N

1 km

150 m

* = seat and sign "Echo Point. Your author is ashamed to admit this was tested by inane shouting....to no avail, apologies to anyone unfortunate enough to hear!

opposite

250 m

200 m

concrete bridge

R i g h

Gle   ann

footbr.

150 m

ends at deep ford

200 m

Sallachail

250 m

Gleann Righ is of geographical interest. It is a flat "hanging valley" rising only 50m in 5km.... exactly 1 in 100 gradient. The valley floor is mostly clear of trees for a width of 200m giving a feeling of being in a tree-enclosed hidden sanctuary. Mountainbikers should note there are many walkers especially in the northern reaches of the woods around Corrychurrachan, so please take care and give way to pedestrians!

The high pass through Lairigmor, forming part of the West Highland Way, runs from the minor public road about 8km south of Fort William to just above Kinlochleven from where it is possible to either join or leave this route, or continue via Loch Eilde Mor into the wilderness area east of the Mamore Forest, with "through route" possibilities all the way to Rannoch, Laggan.... even Dalwhinnie! Refer to the "Link Routes" section at the end of this book.

To Ft. Bill

WHW

Continued Gleann Righ 21

Lundavra

200

Allt na

Meall a Chaorainn 910m

939m

Mullach nan Coirean

opposite

400 m

350 m

300 m

Doire Ban 566m

several sm. fords

250 m

Lairige Moire

Lairigmor

Continued

250 m

350 m

400 m

300 m

350 m

Public Sp. to Callat

Mam na Gualainn

796m

755m

to Loch Leven

24

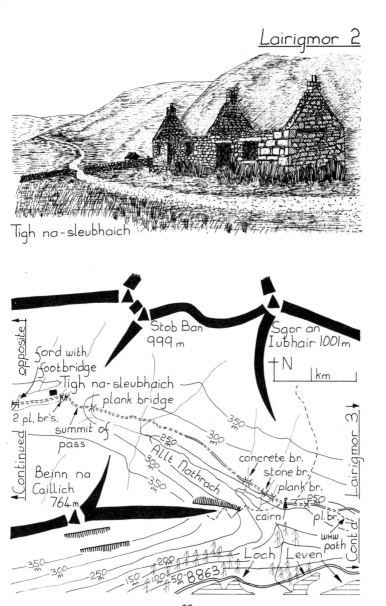

Tigh na-sleubhaich

Stob Ban 999 m

Sgor an Iubhair 1001 m

+ N | km

ford with footbridge

Tigh na-sleubhaich

plank bridge

2 pl. br's.

summit of pass

Allt Nathrach

350 m

300 m

250 m

300 m

350 m

concrete br.

stone br.

plank br.

250 m

cairn

pl. br.

Beinn na Caillich 764 m

WHW path

350 m

300 m

250 m

200 m

150 m

100 m

50 m

B863

Loch Leven

Cont'd

opposite

Continued

Lairigmor 3

25

Lairigmor 3

The environs of Kinlochleven

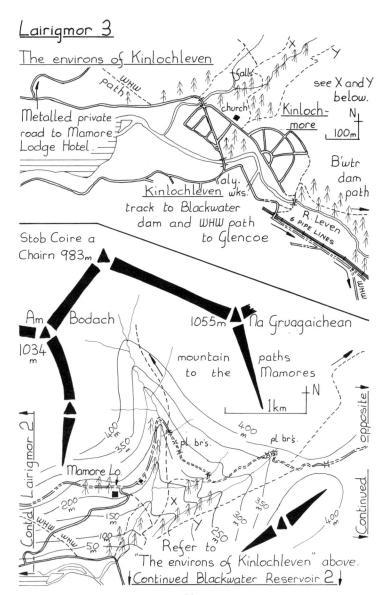

WHW path

see X and Y below.

Metalled private road to Mamore Lodge Hotel.

falls

church

Kinloch-more

N
100m

B'wtr dam path

Kinlochleven aly. wks.

track to Blackwater dam and WHW path to Glencoe

R. Leven
6 PIPE LINES

WHW

Stob Coire a Chairn 983m

Am Bodach

1034 m

1055m

Na Gruagaichean

mountain paths to the Mamores

N
1km

400 m

350 m

pl. br's.

400 m

pl. br's.

Contd Lairigmor 2

Mamore Lo.

200 m

150 m

WHW

100 m

50 m

X

Y

400 m

350 m

300 m

250 m

Continued | opposite

Refer to "The environs of Kinlochleven" above.

Continued Blackwater Reservoir 2

26

Refer to the page opposite for the start of this route as this is shared with the start or end of the Lairigmor track. The two routes form a continuous high traverse, the drop into Kinlochleven being optional by either the West Highland Way path or the Mamore Lodge Hotel road. This route ends at Luibeilt – the Meanach Bothy lies across the Abhainn Rath - a sizeable river. Links with Glen Nevis (not a bike ride) the Lairig Leacach (not a bike ride south of the col) and Loch Treig/Corrour/Ossian (a struggle with a bike as far as Loch Treig) all provide interesting options from Luibeilt, which is 15 km (9.5m) from Kinlochleven by the hotel road or 11 km (7m) by path.

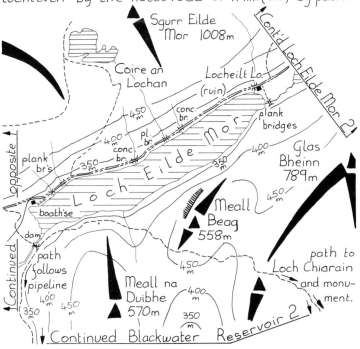

Sgurr Eilde Mor 1008m

Coire an Lochan

Locheilt Lo. (ruin)

Cont'd Loch Eilde Mor 2

conc. br.

plank bridges

450 m

400 m

pl. br.

conc. br.

350 m

Loch Eilde Mor

350 m

400 m

Glas Bheinn 789m

450 m

opposite

plank brs

boath'se

Meall Beag 558m

dam

Continued

path follows pipeline

350 m 400 m 450 m

450 m

Meall na Duibhe 570m

400 m

350 m

path to Loch Chiarain and monument.

Continued Blackwater Reservoir 2

27

Loch Eilde Mor 2

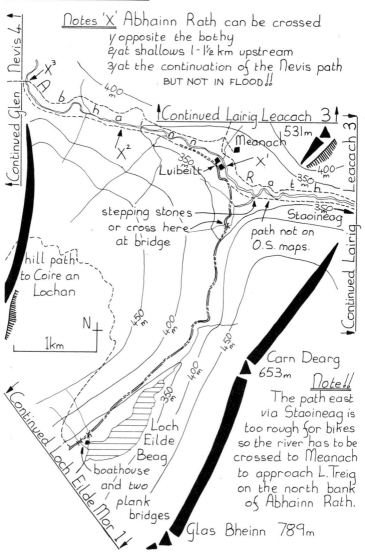

<u>Notes 'X'</u> Abhainn Rath can be crossed
1/ opposite the bothy
2/ at shallows 1-1½ km upstream
3/ at the continuation of the Nevis path
. BUT NOT IN FLOOD!!

Continued Glen Nevis 4

Continued Lairig Leacach 3

531m

Meanach

Luibeilt

stepping stones
or cross here
at bridge

Staoineag

path not on
O.S. maps.

Continued Lairig Leacach 3

hill path
to Coire an
Lochan

N

1km

Continued Lairig Leacach

Carn Dearg
653m

<u>Note!!</u>
The path east
via Staoineag is
too rough for bikes
so the river has to be
crossed to Meanach
to approach L. Treig
on the north bank
of Abhainn Rath.

Loch
Eilde
Beag

boathouse
and two
plank
bridges

Continued Loch Eilde Mor 1

Glas Bheinn 789m

Kinlochleven is often misjudged. Inspection of the town at sea and road level reveals a decaying industrial scene - just the landscape most of us go to Scotland to escape! However less than a mile out of the town in any direction the scene changes to one of wild beauty, whether it be to explore the over populated West Highland Way track to Lairigmor, the Loch Eilde Mor track or one of the three options based on Blackwater Reservoir as follows. One, the West Highland Way south to Glencoe is outside the scope of this book as it is not a 'glen'. The second follows a track to the dam from where there are surprise views of Buachaille Etive Mor to the south and the third is a walkers' path which continues to Loch Treig with a high level connecting path from Loch Eilde Mor (and therefore Lairigmor). This is backpackers' country - the walking distance from Kinlochleven to various points is given below:-

Kinlochleven to:-	
Blackwater dam	6·5km(4m)
The monument	8·5km(5·5m)
Glencoe road (via WHW)	10 km (6m)
Loch Chiarain bothy	11·5km(7·5m)
Loch Treig track	18 km(11·5m)
Staoineag bothy	22km(14m)
Corrour Station (and Morgans Den)	23km(14·5m)
Loch Ossian Youth Hostel	24km(15m)

The 'circular' walk from Kinlochleven via Blackwater Reservoir dam, the monument, and the high level path returning via the outflow of Loch Eilde Mor is about 24km or 15miles.

It should be obvious that the dam, water conduit, and pipelines are firstly potentially dangerous places and secondly strictly private property - view with interest from afar! You have been warned!

Blackwater Reservoir 2

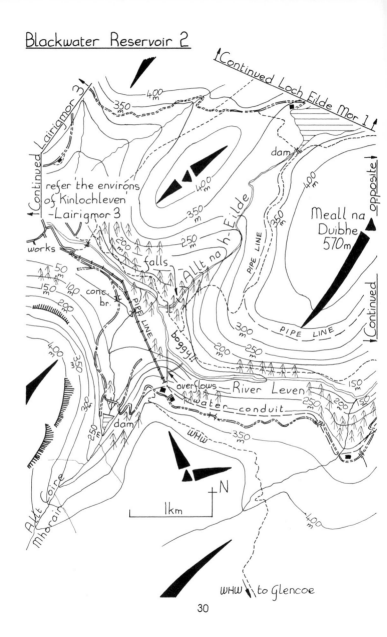

↑Continued Loch Eilde Mor 1↑

←Continued Lairigmor 3

refer the environs
of Kinlochleven
-Lairigmor 3

400 m

350 m

400 m

350 m

400 m

250 m

350 m

250 m

200 m

works

falls

Allt na h-Eilde

dam

Meall na
Duibhe
570m

opposite→

PIPE LINE

50

150

100

conc.
br.

200

PIPE LINE

300 m

250 m

200 m

150

←Continued→

PIPE LINE

boggy!

400 m

350

overflows — River Leven

water conduit

250 m

200

150

250

300

dam

WHW

350 m

400

Allt Coire Mhorair

N

1km

WHW ↓ to Glencoe

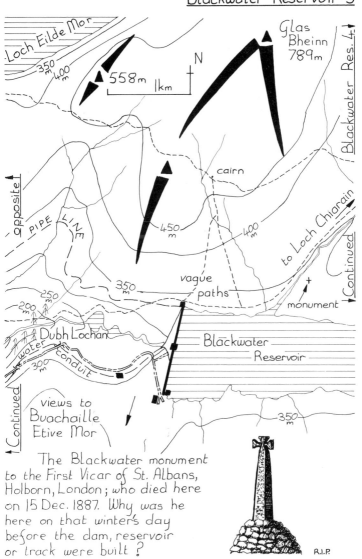

Loch Eilde Mor

350 m
400 m

558 m   1km   N

Glas Bheinn 789m

Blackwater Res. 4

opposite

PIPE LINE

cairn

450 m

400 m

to Loch Chiarain

Continued

350 m

vague paths

monument

250 m
200 m

Dubh Lochan

water conduit

300 m

Blackwater Reservoir

Continued

views to Buachaille Etive Mor

350 m

The Blackwater monument to the First Vicar of St. Albans, Holborn, London; who died here on 15 Dec. 1887. Why was he here on that winter's day before the dam, reservoir or track were built?

R.I.P.

Blackwater Reservoir 4

↑Continued Blackwater Reservoir 5↑

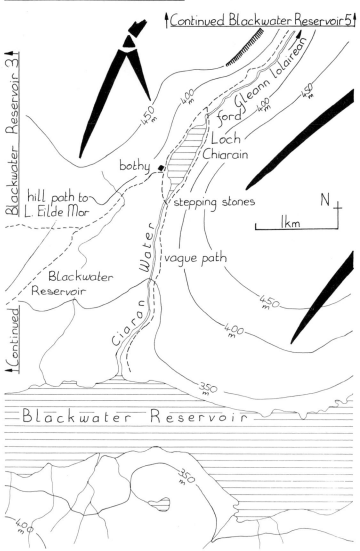

Blackwater Reservoir 3↑

Gleann Iolairean

ford

450 m

400 m

400 m

450 m

Loch Chiarain

bothy

hill path to L. Eilde Mor

stepping stones

N

1km

vague path

Blackwater Reservoir

Ciaran Water

↑Continued

450 m

400 m

350 m

Blackwater Reservoir

350 m

400 m

32

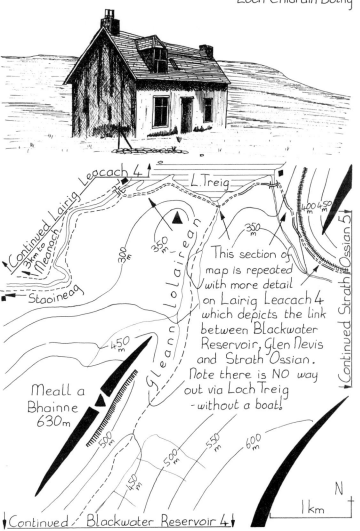

This section of map is repeated with more detail on Lairig Leacach 4 which depicts the link between Blackwater Reservoir, Glen Nevis and Strath Ossian. Note there is NO way out via Loch Treig - without a boat!

Continued Lairig Leacach 4
3km to Meanach

L. Treig

Staoineag

Gleann Iolairean

Meall a Bhainne 630m

Continued Strath Ossian 5

300 m
350 m
350 m
450 m
500 m
450 m
500 m
550 m
600 m
400 m
450 m

N

1 km

Continued Blackwater Reservoir 4

Glen Nevis 1

Glen Nevis is included almost into the centre of Fort William despite a public road running for 10km (6m) into the glen. The reason for this is to illustrate the forest track which relieves the walker of at least 6km (4m) of metalled road. I say walker because although the forest track is ideal for a mountainbike it would be folly to carry a bike up Glen Nevis, the gorge is a dangerous place for the unwary and the continuing path is rough. The cyclists' route to the wilds of Rannoch Moor lies over Lairigmor and by Loch Eilde Mor. Glen Nevis has the dubious distinction of being the wettest place in the UK, the Water of Nevis is a major river – but only 20km long! It drops 400m in its turbulent length, a 100m drop in the Nevis Gorge alone. Sadly there is no shelter between Fort William and Meanach bothy some 23km or 15m distant. The glen provides access not only to Rannoch Moor but also to Ben Nevis, the Aonachs, the Grey Corries and to the south the Mamores. The flat watershed, watched over by a drumlin with a name - Tom-an Eite-leads into the un-named glen down which the Abhainn Rath flows into Loch Treig and from which paths lead north via the Lairig Leacach to Spean Bridge.

Fort William has in recent years suffered badly from the incurable disease of "citycentreitis"-usually spread by planners and nicknamed 'progress'. Complete with bypass, subways, masses of concrete, infected with mindless architecture, it now suffers the common symptoms of graffiti, vandalism, litter and worse. The day planners learn that the built environment influences behaviour will be a great day for all. Get on with it man - this is a guide book!! (Your author now feels much better with that off his chest and will now proceed up the glen with a map!)

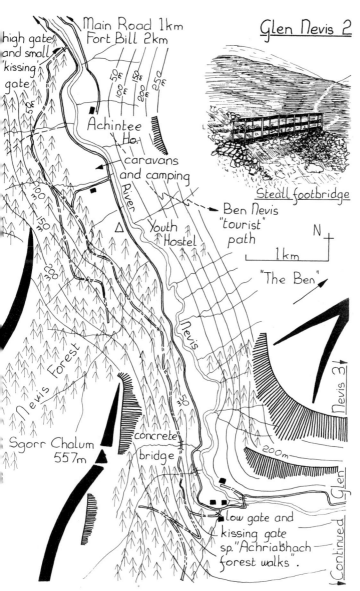

Main Road 1km
Fort Bill 2km

Glen Nevis 2

high gate and small 'kissing' gate

50m 100m 150m 200m 250m

Achintee Ho.

caravans and camping

Steall footbridge

Ben Nevis "tourist" path

Youth Hostel

N

1km

"The Ben"

Nevis Forest

Nevis

Glen Nevis 3

Sgorr Chalum 557m

concrete bridge

200m

low gate and kissing gate sp. "Achriabhach forest walks".

(Continued Glen

35

Glen Nevis 3

The "bridge" to the climbing hut.

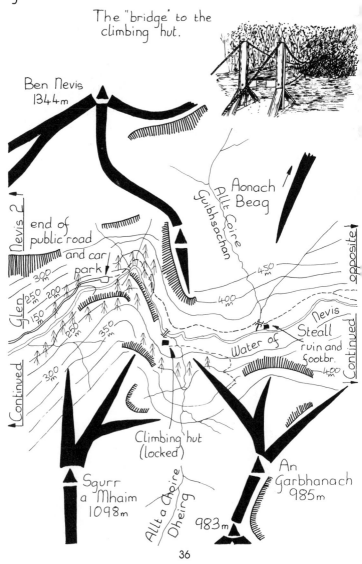

Ben Nevis
1344m

Glen Nevis 2

end of public road and car park

Aonach Beag

Allt Coire Guibhsachan

450 m

400 m

300 m
250 m
200 m
150 m

200 m

350 m

300 m

Water of Nevis

Steall ruin and footbr.

400 m

opposite

Continued

Continued

Climbing hut
(locked)

Sgurr a Mhaim
1098m

Allt a Choire Dheirg

983m

An Garbhanach
985m

36

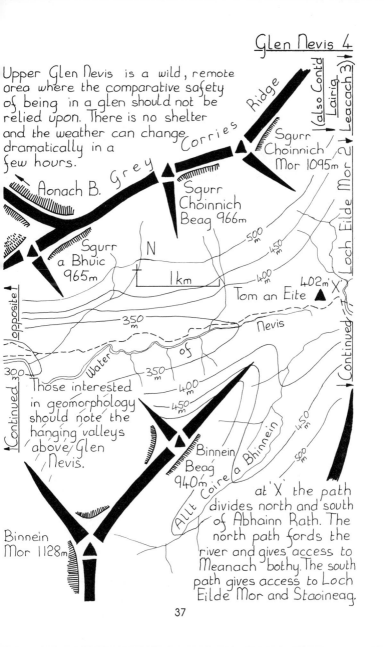

Upper Glen Nevis is a wild, remote area where the comparative safety of being in a glen should not be relied upon. There is no shelter and the weather can change dramatically in a few hours.

Grey Corries Ridge

(also Cont'd Lairig Leacach 3)

Sgurr Choinnich Mor 1095m

Aonach B.

Sgurr Choinnich Beag 966m

Loch Eilde Mor 2

Sgurr a Bhuic 965m

N

500m
450m
400m

Tom an Eite   402m X

1 km

opposite

350m

Nevis

of

Water

350m
400m
450m

Continued 300m

Continued

Those interested in geomorphology should note the hanging valleys above Glen Nevis.

Binnein Beag 940m

Allt Coire a Bhinnein

450m
500m

Binnein Mor 1128m

at 'X' the path divides north and south of Abhainn Rath. The north path fords the river and gives access to Meanach bothy. The south path gives access to Loch Eilde Mor and Staoineag.

Leanachan Forest 1

Leanachan Forest extends from Torlundy, 4km N.E. of Fort William, to the Lairig Leacach track 3km east of Spean Bridge. However, The Cour which drains the northern aspect of the Grey Corries and the eastern aspect of the Aonachs prevents travel further east except by road. The entire area is bicycle friendly and, apart from the skiers' access road being "over the top" the area has been developed with conservation in mind, not repeating the horrendous environmental damage seen (all too clearly!) at Cairngorm. We must thank the Forestry Commission for encouraging cycling. The old British Aluminium railway forms the basis for some tracks but is otherwise shown thus:- ++++

The adits and various structures, dams etc. associated with the B.A. hydro scheme are strictly private and must be regarded as out of bounds.

Cyclists are warned regarding the speed of traffic on the ski access road. Cars with skis on the roof travel much faster than normal cars, and given a new stretch of road the speed often approaches lunacy.

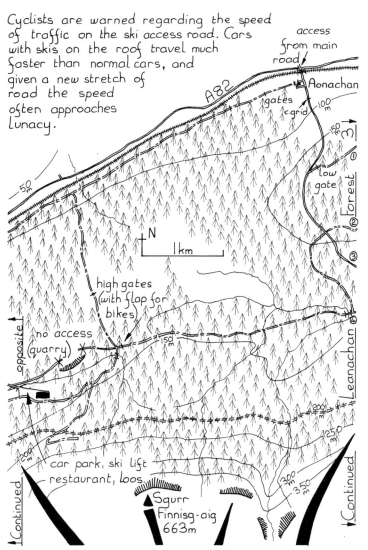

access from main road

Aonachan

gates

c.grid

100 m

150 m

Forest

③

low gate

②

③

A82

50 m

N

1 km

high gates (with flap for bikes)

no access (quarry)

150 m

opposite

Leanachan

④

200 m

250 m

200 m

300 m

car park, ski lift restaurant, loos

Sgurr Finnisg-aig 663m

300 m

350 m

Continued

Continued

39

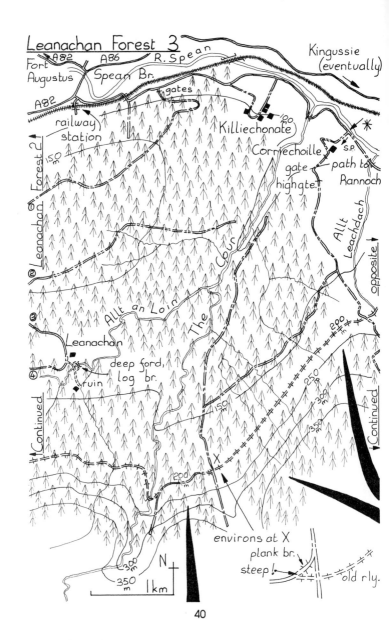

Leanachan Forest 3

Kingussie (eventually)

A82 A86 R. Spean

Fort Augustus

Spean Br.

A82

railway station

gates

Killiechonate

Corriechoille

s.p.

gate path to

highgte Rannoch

Leanachan Forest 2

150 m

Allt Leachdach

The Cour

opposite

Allt an Loin

200 m

Leanachan

deep ford, log br.

ruin

250

300

150 m

350

Continued

Continued

X

200 m

environs at X

plank br.

steep!

old rly.

350 m

350 m 1km

N

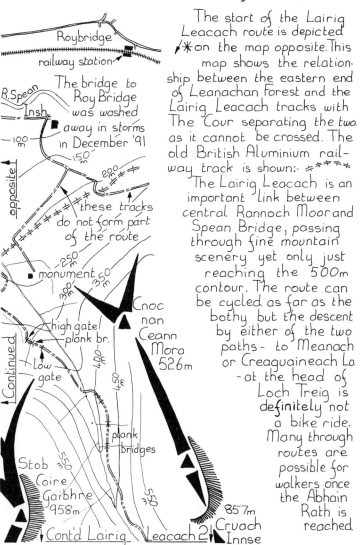

The start of the Lairig Leacach route is depicted /✳ on the map opposite. This map shows the relationship between the eastern end of Leanachan Forest and the Lairig Leacach tracks with The Cour separating the two as it cannot be crossed. The old British Aluminium railway track is shown :- ✳✳✳✳✳

The Lairig Leacach is an important link between central Rannoch Moor and Spean Bridge, passing through fine mountain scenery yet only just reaching the 500m contour. The route can be cycled as far as the bothy but the descent by either of the two paths - to Meanach or Creaguaineach Lo - at the head of Loch Treig is definitely not a bike ride. Many through routes are possible for walkers once the Abhain Rath is reached.

Map labels:

Roybridge
railway station

The bridge to Roy Bridge was washed away in storms in December '91

R.Spean
Insh
-100 m
150
200
opposite

these tracks do not form part of the route

250
monument
300
350

Cnoc nan Ceann Mora 526m

high gate
plank br.
400
Low gate
450

plank bridges

Stob Coire Gaibhre 958m
350
550
550
350

857m
Cruach Innse

Cont'd Lairig Leacach 2

Lairig Leacach 2

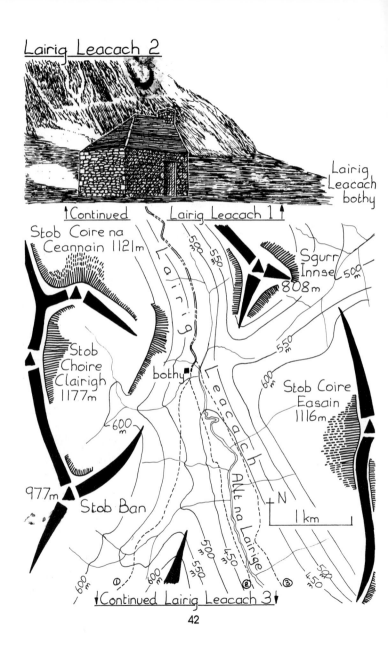

Lairig Leacach bothy

↑Continued Lairig Leacach 1 ↑

Stob Coire na Ceannain 1121m

Sgurr Innse 808m

Stob Choire Clairigh 1177m

bothy

Stob Coire Easain 1116m

500 m

550 m

600 m

Lairig Leacach

Allt na Lairige

977m

Stob Ban

N

1 km

600 m

500 m

450 m

550 m

① ② ③

↓Continued Lairig Leacach 3 ↓

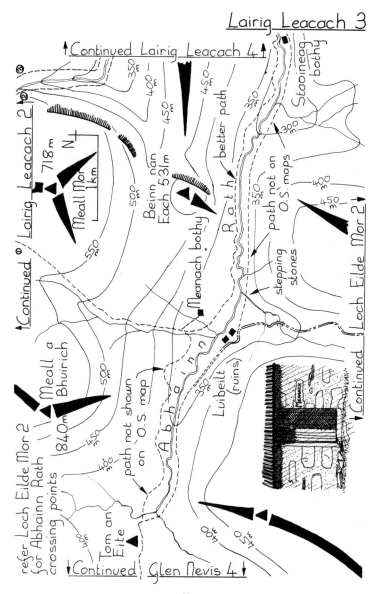

↑ Continued Lairig Leacach 4 ↑

↑ Continued Lairig Leacach 2 ↑

Staoineag bothy

718 m

N

Meall Mor
1 km

Beinn nan Each 531 m

better path

350 m

400 m

450 m

450 m

300

↑ Continued ⑥ Lairig Leacach 2 ↑

500 m

550 m

Meanach bothy

path not on O.S. maps

400 m

450 m

Loch Eilde Mor 2

500 m

450 m

stepping stones

350 m

Meall a Bhuirich

840 m

path not shown on O.S. map

A b h a i n n   R a t h

Luibeilt (ruins)

Continued Loch Eilde Mor 2 →

MEANACH

refer Loch Eilde Mor 2 for Abhainn Rath crossing points

400 m

450 m

path not shown on O.S. map

400 m

Tom an Eite

400 m

450 m

↓ Continued Glen Nevis 4 ↓

43

Lairig Leacach 4

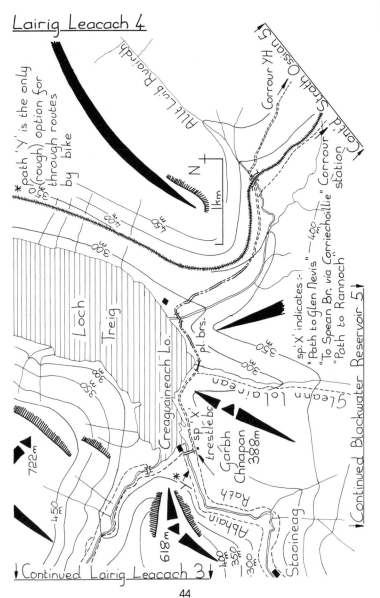

Corrour YH

Cont'd Strath Ossian 5

Allt Luib Ruaridh

N

1km

* path 'y' is the only (rough) option for through routes by bike

400m
450m
300m

Loch Treig

350m
300m

722m

450m

350m
300m

450m

619

Abhain Rath

Creaguaineach Lo.

pl. brs.

Gleann Lolairean

sp.'X' trestle br.

Garbh Chnapan 388m

400m
350m
300m

Staoineag

350m

300m

sp. 'X' indicates :-
"Path to Glen Nevis"
"To Spean Br. via Corriechoillie" Corrour station
"Path to Rannoch"

Corrour station

↓Continued Lairig Leacach 3↓

←Continued Blackwater Reservoir 5

44

Staoineag

West from
Staoineag

Bridge, Loch Treig

West of Drumochter

West of Drumochter

Access:- Access to the routes included in this section is either south of the A86 Fort William to Kingussie road or west of the A9 as it passes over Drumochter. The railway station at Dalwhinnie can be used for numerous long distance backpacking treks via Ben Alder Forest to Loch Ossian or south to Rannoch. Close study of this book is necessary as many through routes are not suitable for mountainbikes, the exceptions being L.Ericht/Pattack/Lochan na h.Earba/L.Ossian; and L.Garry/Duinish.

Accommodation:- Outwith Kingussie, which has hotels, B and B's, a youth hostel and campsite, accommodation is sparse. At Corrour is a bunkhouse and a (usually fully booked) youth hostel. The start of each route may be reached by car but an enforced return to the same point each day can be a severe limitation.

Geographical Features:- Dominated by the Ben Alder and Aonach Beag mountain groups much of the area comprises wild moors and rounded hills. Scenically the River Pattock wins the contest in the variety of landscape presented at each turn in the glen, whilst for wild grandeur the area between Loch Pattack, Loch Ericht and Strath Ossian is unbeaten.

Mountains:- Ben Alder reigns supreme, its south eastern face drops steeply to form some four miles of shoreline of Loch Ericht. Ben Alder is a serious undertaking and is often tackled by using a bike as far as Culra and then continuing on foot, an expedition for the very fit only!! Aonach Beag, almost as high and just as remote has the same access problems as Ben Alder, "problems" that are indeed the main attraction of these remote heights. Beinn a Chlachair, another fine summit just N. of An Lairig deserves a mention as also the more rounded 'Munro's' of Dalnaspidal Forest to the east

Rivers:- Scottish rivers have a habit of changing their names repeatedly - often without reason! Their description is therefore confusing. However, the star of this region is the River Pattack, only so named below Loch Pattack. Higher up Allt Cam and Allt Bhealaich Dhuibh which becomes Allt a Chaoil-reidhe feed the loch. Loch Ossian and its River Ossian becomes the Abhain Ghuilbinn before joining the River Spean which joins the dammed and natural sections of Loch Laggan. The region's water ends up in the Spey, Spean and Tay.

Forests:- Large areas of forest extend to the north of Strath Ossian from Fersit to Moy. At Ardverikie are both beautiful mixed woodland and commercial forestry. Further commercial planting extends the Loch Ericht forests north of Dalwhinnie. New (1993) forest roads have been laid but these are generally short from their numerous roadside starting points and do not provide worthwhile walks or bike rides. The small pockets of natural woodland, mostly birch, add much interest especially alongside the Pattack.

Lochs:- Loch Ericht, nearly 20 miles long and with a dam at each end is by far the largest in the region. Fed with water borrowed from the other side of the River Truim via the Loch Cuaich aqueduct (see Book 2, The Atholl Glens), Loch Ericht serves a power station at Bridge of Ericht. Loch Garry lies between the wilds of Dalnaspidal Forest and feeds the River Garry. Loch Errochty, another hydro scheme provides several tracks around its dam. Of the mountain lochs Loch Pattack is the largest and many of the corries high on Ben Alder, Aonach Beag and Beinn a Chlach-air hold lochans. Lochan na h-Earba lies above the natural and dammed Loch Laggan forming the north limit of the region whilst Loch Ossian lies at the centre of Rannoch Moor with many excellent routes converging around its wild shores.

Emergency:- There are public telephones at or near the start of each route except at Moy. Between these points and the Hostel/station at Corrour there is nothing, so it is vital to take all the usual precautions including leaving word of your intended route.

West of Drumochter Routes 1

Strath Ossian

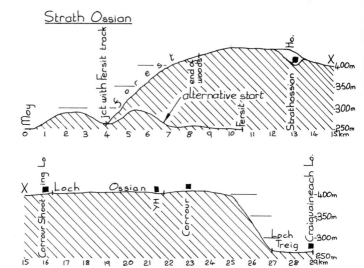

Corrour to Craiguaineach Lo
is included to illustrate the
drop to (or climb from) L. Treig.

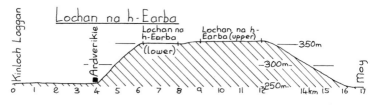

Lochan na h-Earba

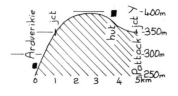

Note:-

1/ Ardverikie to Pattack
Link track to 'Y' opposite.

2/ Loch Laggan lochside
track not included as it is
flat :- "_____" for 13km.

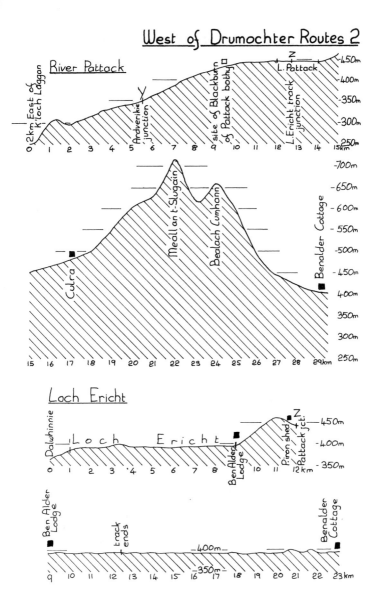

West of Drumochter Routes 3

Loch Garry

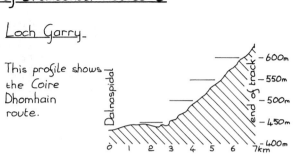

This profile shows the Coire Dhomhain route.

The Loch Garry lochside track is flat apart from a 30m climb to Duinish Bridge (7km from Dalnaspidal) and a 20m drop to Duinish (8km from Dalnaspidal)

Loch Errochty

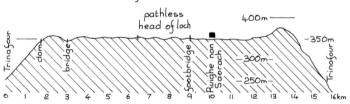

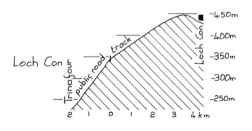

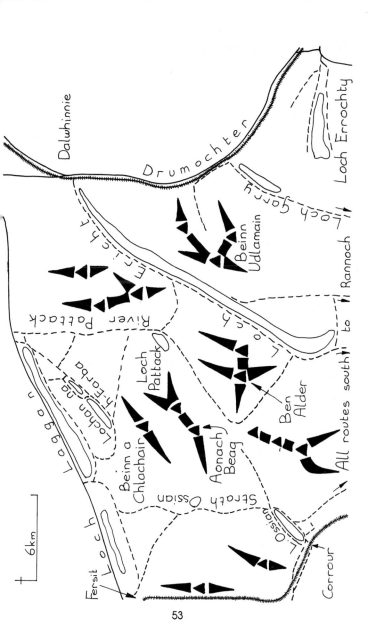

Dalwhinnie

Drumochter

Loch Errochty

Loch Garry

Beinn Udlamain

River Pattack

Loch Ericht

to Rannoch

Loch Laggan

Lochan na h'Earba

Loch Pattack

Loch Ericht

Ben Alder

All routes south to

Beinn a Chlachain

Aonach Beag

Strath Ossian

Loch Ossian

Corrour

Loch Treig

Fersit

6km

53

The Environs of Fersit 1

Fersit may be easily dismissed as just an alternative 'start' to Strath Ossian and the long glen would not leave sufficient time for the exploration of Fersit. However there is much to interest the intrepid explorer. The dams and adits belong to British Aluminium and should be regarded as out of bounds.

The old British Aluminium railway is shown:- ⊁⊁⊁⊁⊁
Any detailed exploration of this must be with the permission of British Aluminium in Fort Bill.

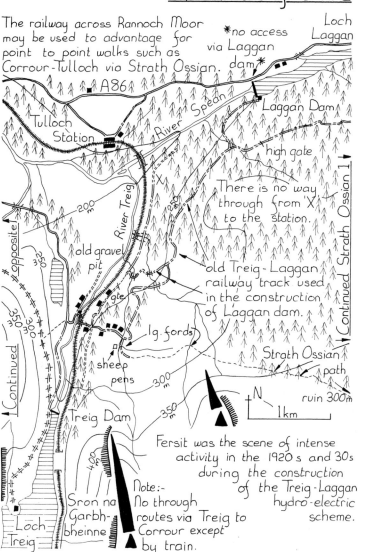

The railway across Rannoch Moor may be used to advantage for point to point walks such as Corrour-Tulloch via Strath Ossian.

Loch Laggan

no access via Laggan dam

A86

Tulloch Station

River Spean

Laggan Dam

high gate

X

There is no way through from 'X' to the station.

River Treig

old gravel pit

old Treig-Laggan railway track used in the construction of Laggan dam.

gte

lg. fords

sheep pens

Strath Ossian path

ruin 300m

N

1km

200

250

350

300

300

350

400

#opposite

#Continued

Continued Strath Ossian 1

Treig Dam

Sron na Garbh-bheinne

Note:- No through routes via Treig to Corrour except by train.

Fersit was the scene of intense activity in the 1920s and 30s during the construction of the Treig-Laggan hydro-electric scheme.

Loch Treig

55

Strath Ossian is unique. No other route passes through a long, wild glen and yet has a youth hostel, a bunkhouse and a railway station at its head. Strath Ossian is also well connected to neighbouring glens — Nevis, Rannoch, Pattack and the Lairig Leacach. The presence of both accommodation and public transport at Corrour opens up a multitude of 2-3 day backpacking options for the walker and through routes for the long distance off-road cyclist. The severity of winter on the moor and its glens needs to be repeated. People have died on Rannoch Moor. After that cheering thought, the rewards for the fit and experienced are to be at one with the landscape, the peace and the solitude — at least until the next train is due!

* no access via the dam *

to Fort William

A86

River Spean

Laggan Dam

conc. br.

high gate

300m

Allt Loraich

Continued Fersit 2

Continued opposite

N

1 km

250m

to Fersit

fords

250m

350m

Cont'd Strath Ossian 4

ruin

Distances from the A86 at Moy are as follows:-
Jct. of forest rd. from Fersit 4km (2·5m)
End of forest 8·5 km (5m)
Strathossian House 12·5 km (7·5m)
Corrour Shooting Lodge 16 km (10m)
Loch Ossian Youth Hostel 22 km (13·5m)
Corrour station 23 km (14·5m)
Loch Treig 27 km (17m)
For Fersit add 3km (2m), for Tulloch station add 8km (5m).

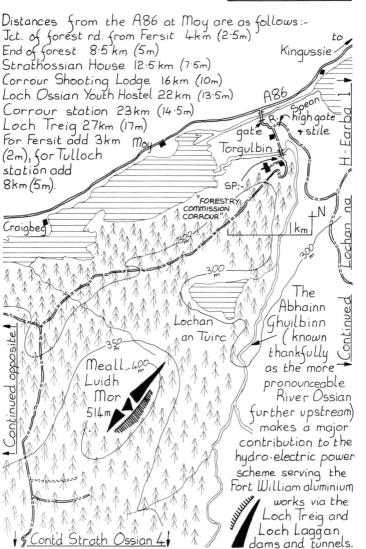

to Kingussie

A86

Spean high gate + stile

I.R. gate

Torgulbin

SP:-

"FORESTRY COMMISSION CORROUR"

Moy

Craigbeg

N

1km

300m

300m

300m

Lochan an Tuirc

Lochan na H. Earba

Continued

Meall Luidh Mor
350m
400m
514m

The Abhainn Ghuilbinn (known thankfully as the more pronounceable River Ossian further upstream) makes a major contribution to the hydro-electric power scheme serving the Fort William aluminium works via the Loch Treig and Loch Laggan dams and tunnels.

← Continued opposite

↓ Cont'd Strath Ossian 4 ↓

Strath Ossian 3

Strathossian House

Corrour
station;
Morgan's Den
bunkhouse is
situated at
the south
end of the
platform.

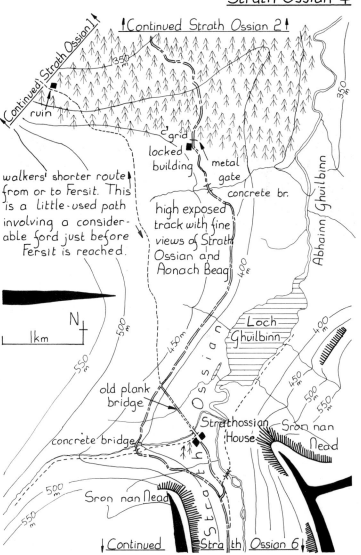

↑Continued Strath Ossian 2↑

←Continued Strath Ossian 1

350m

ruin

'c' grid

locked
building

metal
gate

concrete br.

walkers' shorter route
from or to Fersit. This
is a little-used path
involving a consider-
able ford just before
Fersit is reached.

high exposed
track with fine
views of Strath
Ossian and
Aonach Beag

350m

Abhainn Ghuilbinn

N

1km

500m

400m

Loch
Ghuilbinn

400m

450m

550m

450m

500m

550m

old plank
bridge

Sron nan
Nead

concrete bridge

Strathossian
House

500m

550m

Sron nan Nead

Strath Ossian

↓Continued   Strath Ossian 6↓

Strath Ossian 5

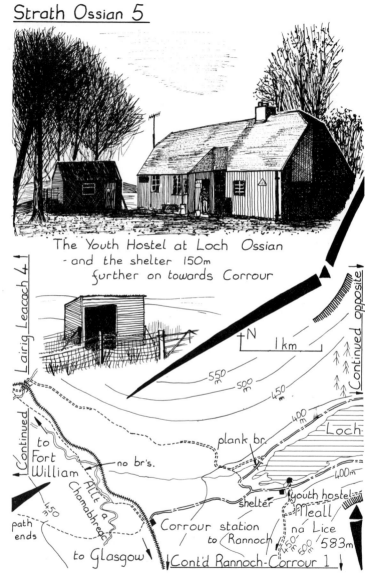

The Youth Hostel at Loch Ossian
- and the shelter 150m
further on towards Corrour

Lairig Leacach 4↑

Continued opposite →

N   1km

550 m
500 m
450

Continued

to
Fort
William ←

no br's.

Allt a Chomabhreac

450 m

path ends

to Glasgow ↓

plank br.

shelter

Corrour station
to Rannoch →

400 m

400m

Loch

youth hostel
Meall na Lice 583m

450 m   500 m

↓ Cont'd Rannoch-Corrour 1 ↓

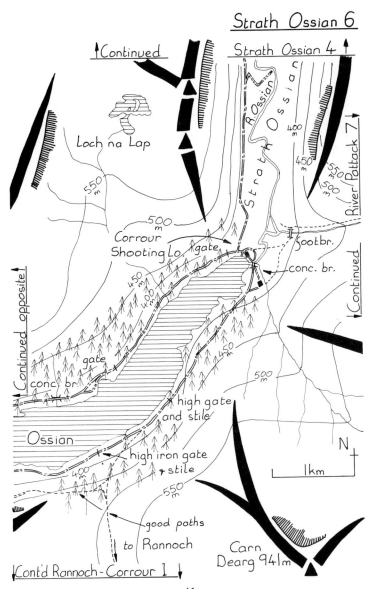

Continued

R. Ossian

Strath Ossian

River Pattack 7

Loch na Lap

550 m

500 m

450 m

500 m

450 m

500 m

Corrour
Shooting Lo. gate

footbr.

conc. br.

Continued opposite

Continued

450 m

400 m

gate

450 m

500 m

conc. br.

Ossian

high gate
and stile

high iron gate
+ stile

400 m

550 m

N

1km

good paths
to Rannoch

Carn
Dearg 941m

Cont'd Rannoch-Corrour 1

Lochan na h-Earba 1

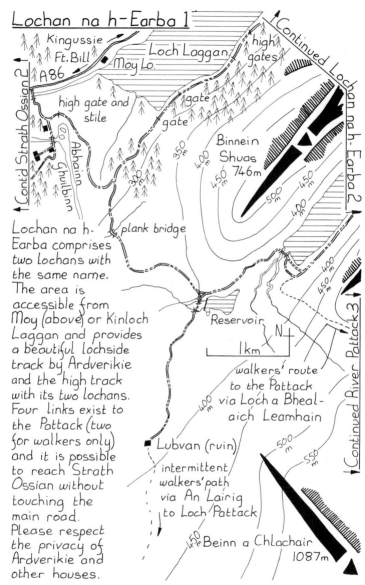

Kingussie →
Ft.Bill
Moy Lo.
A86
Loch Laggan
high gates

Continued Lochan na h-Earba 2

← Contd Strath Ossian 2

high gate and stile
gate
gate
gate

Abhainn Ghuilbinn

Binnein Shuas 746m

350m
400m
450m
500m
450m
400m

plank bridge

Lochan na h-Earba comprises two lochans with the same name. The area is accessible from Moy (above) or Kinloch Laggan and provides a beautiful lochside track by Ardverikie and the high track with its two lochans. Four links exist to the Pattack (two for walkers only) and it is possible to reach Strath Ossian without touching the main road. Please respect the privacy of Ardverikie and other houses.

Reservoir

N

1 km

400m
450m

Continued River Pattack 3 →

walkers' route to the Pattack via Loch a Bhealaich Leamhain

400m

Lubvan (ruin)

intermittent walkers' path via An Lairig to Loch Pattack

500m
550m

450m
Beinn a Chlachair
1087m

62

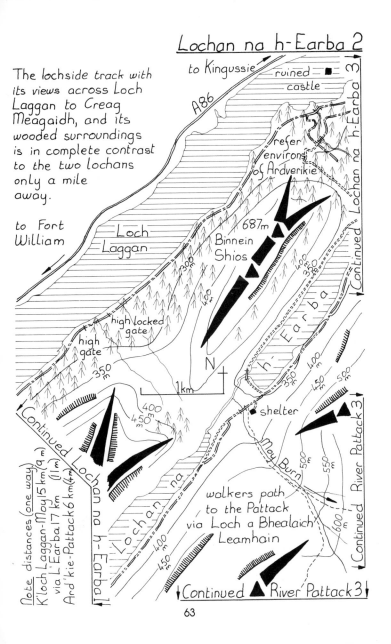

to Kingussie

ruined castle

A86

refer environs of Ardverikie

Lochan na h-Earba 3

to Fort William

Loch Laggan

687m

Binnein Shios

400m

300m

350m

Continued Lochan na h-Earba 3

high locked gate

high gate

350m

N

1km

400m

450m

shelter

Moy Burn

400m

350m
450m
500m

Lochan na

walkers path to the Pattack via Loch a Bhealaich Leamhain

500m

550m

600m

Continued River Pattack 3

400m

450m

The lochside track with its views across Loch Laggan to Creag Meagaidh, and its wooded surroundings is in complete contrast to the two lochans only a mile away.

Note distances (one way)
K'loch Laggan-Moy 15 km (9 m)
via L'Earba 17 km (11m)
Ard'kie-Pattack 6 km (4m)

Continued Lochan na h-Earba 1

↓ Continued ➤ River Pattack 3 ↓

63

Lochan na h - Earba 3

Access from Kinloch Laggan is by the rather imposing bridge and lodge. Approaches from Moy and the River Pattack tracks are less intrusive.

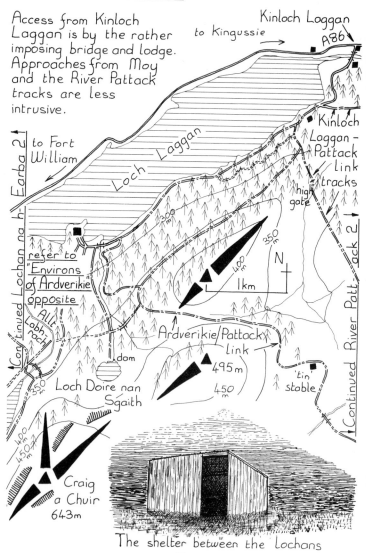

to Kingussie

Kinloch Laggan

A86

to Fort William

Loch Laggan

Kinloch Laggan - Pattack link tracks

high gate

to Kinloch Laggan na h - Earba 2

refer to "Environs of Ardverikie" opposite

Allt Labh roch

N

1km

350m

400m

Continued River Pattack 2

dam

Ardverikie/Pattack link

Loch Doire nan Sgaith

495m

450m

'tin' stable

Continued River Pattack 2

Continued Lochan na h - Earba 2

350m

400m
450m

Craig a Chuir
643m

The shelter between the Lochans

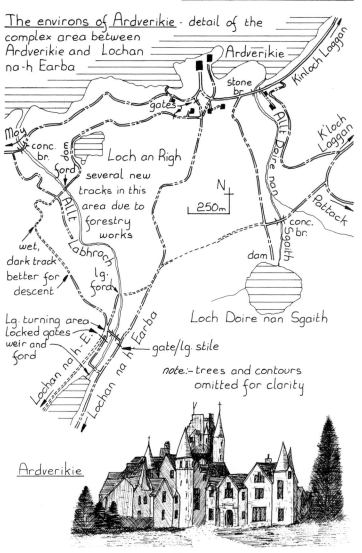

The environs of Ardverikie - detail of the complex area between Ardverikie and Lochan na-h Earba

Ardverikie

Kinloch Laggan

stone br.

gates

Moy

conc. br.

E dam

ford

Loch an Righ

several new tracks in this area due to forestry works

Allt Doire nan

K'loch Laggan

Pattack

conc. br.

Sgaith

N
250m

Allt Labhrach

wet, dark track better for descent

lg. ford

dam

Loch Doire nan Sgaith

Lg. turning area
locked gates
weir and ford

Lochan nah-E.

Lochan na h Earba

gate/lg. stile

Lochan na h Earba

note:- trees and contours omitted for clarity

Ardverikie

River Pattack 1

This route should be called Glen Pattack but no such name exists, so River Pattack will suffice. The glen is beautiful with deep wooded gorges, waterfalls, Loch Pattack and the promise of the wilds of Ben Alder and Aonach Beag ahead. Mountain bike access is only viable as far as Culra bothy, or the superb through route by Loch Ericht to Dalwhinnie, or via Lochan na h-Earba to Moy and Strath Ossian. For the backpacker there is even more scope with paths taking a more direct route to Lochan na h-Earba; a pathless connection via An Lairig to Strath Ossian; and good paths to Benalder Cottage, and from this yet another through route to Strath Ossian. These long distance routes are very committing and adequate safety precautions should be taken. The waters of the Pattack end up generating electricity in Fort William for British Aluminium. There is shelter at Culra but Blackburn of Pattack bothy was burnt down. It is difficult to avoid the attention of the ponies near the 'iron shed'.

Culra-the smoke is imaginary, there is no wood for miles !!

Culra footbridge

Pattack 'iron shed'

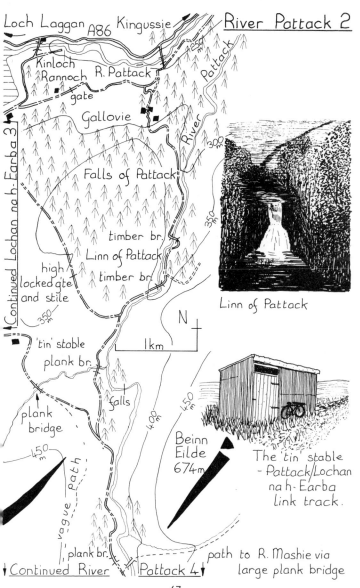

Loch Laggan A86 Kingussie

Kinloch
Rannoch R. Pattack
gate
Gallovie

River Pattack

250 m

300

Continued Lochan na h-Earba 3

Falls of Pattack

350

timber br.
Linn of Pattack
timber br.

high
locked gate
and stile

350 m

Linn of Pattack

'tin' stable
plank br.

N

1km

plank
bridge

450 m

falls

400 m

450 m

vague Path

Beinn
Eilde
674m

The 'tin' stable
– Pattack/Lochan
na h-Earba
link track.

plank br.

Continued River Pattack 4 path to R. Mashie via
large plank bridge

River Pattack 3

The walkers paths depicted below are not strictly 'glen' routes but the close proximity of Loch Pattack and Lochan na h-Earba warrants their inclusion.

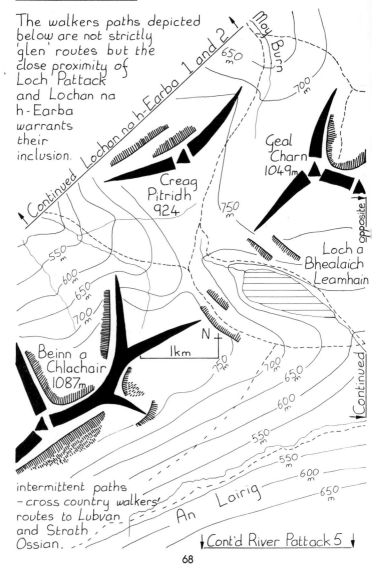

Continued Lochan na h-Earba 1 and 2

Moy Burn

650 m

700 m

Continued Lochan na h-Earba 1 and 2

Creag Pitridh 924

750 m

Geal Charn 1049m

Loch a Bhealaich Leamhain

opposite

550 m

600 m

650 m

700 m

N

1km

Beinn a Chlachair 1087m

750 m

700 m

650 m

600 m

Continued

550 m

550 m

600 m

650 m

intermittent paths - cross country walkers' routes to Lubvan and Strath Ossian.

An Lairig

Cont'd River Pattack 5

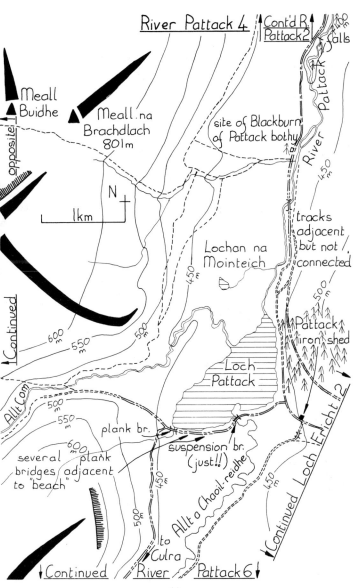

River Pattack 4

Meall Buidhe

Meall na Brachdlach 801m

opposite!

N

1km

Continued

Allt Coire

600m
550m
500m

500m
550m
plank br.

600m

several plank bridges adjacent to "beach"

500m

450m

to Culra

River Pattack 6

Cont'd R. Pattack 2

falls

River Pattack

site of Blackburn of Pattack bothy

450m

tracks adjacent but not connected

Lochan na Mointeich

450m

500m

Pattack iron shed

Loch Pattack

suspension br. (just!!)

to Allt a Chaoil-reidhe

450m

Continued Loch Ericht 2

Continued

River Pattack 5

The map below depicts the high level walkers path over Bealach Dubh and Bealach Chumhainn to Benalder Cottage on the shore of Loch Ericht. The path is a 'made' pony track and, if rideable link routes were to be found beyond the cottage, could just about be described as a hard through cycle route. However both the lochside track NE along Loch Ericht and the path SW of Benalder Cottage are unsuitable for cycles due to rough terrain, bogs etc. Also cycles are disallowed on Camusericht Estate. Refer "South West Loch Ericht" for details.

River Pattack 3

River Pattack

Continued

Aonach Beag
1114m

1132m

N   1km

Beinn Eibhinn

750
m

750
m

Meall an t-

Slugain

intermittent path
does not make it
to the high path!

Continued opposite

refer to the
Pattack/ Ossian
link on R. Pattack

600
m

no link !!

700
m

Cont'd River
Pattack 7

Uisge Labhair

600
m

650
m

700
m

to Benalder
Cottage

Bealach Chum-
hainn

Loch Ericht 4

Beinn a
Chumhainn 901m

Cont'd

70

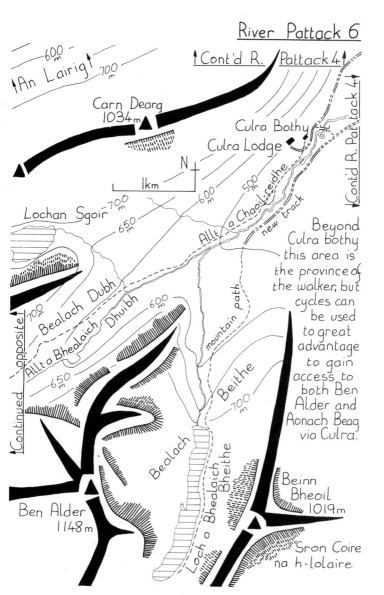

600 m

↑An Lairig↑   700 m

↑Cont'd R. Pattack 4↑

Carn Dearg 1034m

Culra Bothy

Culra Lodge

N

1km

Lochan Sgoir   700 m

650 m

Allt a Chaoil-reidhe

500 m

600 m

new track

↓Cont'd R. Pattack 4↓

Beyond Culra bothy this area is the province of the walker, but cycles can be used to great advantage to gain access to both Ben Alder and Aonach Beag via Culra.

Bealach Dubh

Allt a Bhealaich Dhuibh

600 m

700 m

←Continued opposite

650 m

mountain path

Beithe

700 m

Bealach

Loch a Bhealaich Bheithe

Ben Alder 1148m

Beinn Bheoil 1019m

Sron Coire na h-Iolaire

River Pattack 7

Pattack/Ossian Link

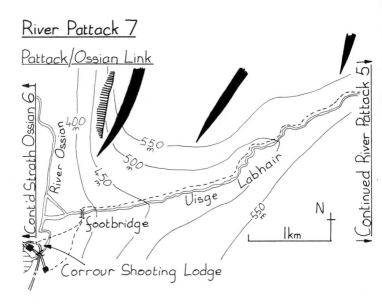

The shaky suspension bridge at Loch Pattack

<u>Table of one-way distances</u> from the A86 N. of
Gallovie to :- Loch Pattack (sus.br.)   13·5 km (8·5m)
     Culra bothy   17 km (11m)
     Corrour shooting Lo.   31 km (19·5m)
     Benalder Cottage   29 km (17m)
     Ben Alder Lo. (Loch Ericht)   15 km (9·5m)
     Dalwhinnie   25 km (15·5m)

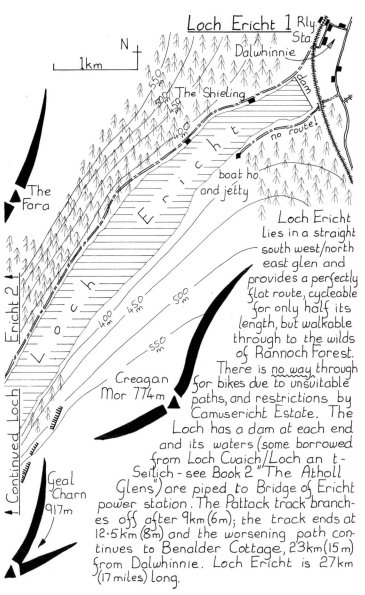

Loch Ericht 1

Rly. Sta.

Dalwhinnie

N

1km

The Shieling

550 m

500 m

450 m

400 m

dam

no route!

boat ho. and jetty

L o c h   E r i c h t

The Fora

Ericht 2

Continued Loch

400 m

450 m

500 m

550 m

Creagan Mor 774 m

Geal Charn 917 m

Loch Ericht lies in a straight south west/north east glen and provides a perfectly flat route, cycleable for only half its length, but walkable through to the wilds of Rannoch Forest. There is no way through for bikes due to unsuitable paths, and restrictions by Camusericht Estate. The Loch has a dam at each end and its waters (some borrowed from Loch Cuaich/Loch an t-Seilich – see Book 2 "The Atholl Glens") are piped to Bridge of Ericht power station. The Pattack track branches off after 9km (6m); the track ends at 12·5km (8m) and the worsening path continues to Benalder Cottage, 23km (15 m) from Dalwhinnie. Loch Ericht is 27km (17 miles) long.

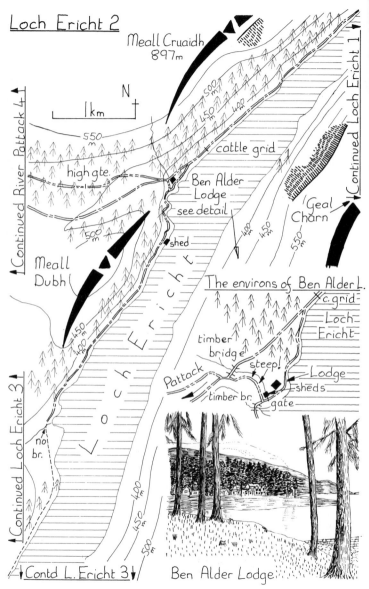

Loch Ericht 2

Meall Cruaidh
897m

Continued Loch Ericht 1

Continued River Pattack 4

N

1 km

550 m

cattle grid

high gte.

Ben Alder
Lodge
see detail

Geal
Charn

shed

400 m   450   550
m

Meall
Dubh

450 m   400

Loch Ericht

The environs of Ben Alder L.

c. grid

Loch
Ericht

timber
bridge

steep!

Pattack

Lodge
sheds

timber br.

gate

Continued Loch Ericht 3

no
br.

0

V

400
450
500 m

Contd L. Ericht 3

Ben Alder Lodge

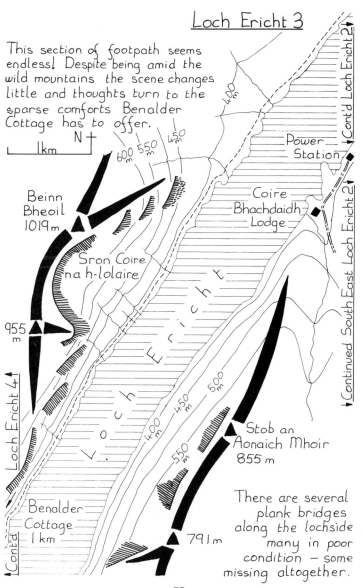

This section of footpath seems endless! Despite being amid the wild mountains the scene changes little and thoughts turn to the sparse comforts Benalder Cottage has to offer.

N

1km

600m 550m 450m

Cont'd Loch Ericht 2

400m

Power Station

Beinn Bheoil 1019m

Coire Bhachdaidh Lodge

Sron Coire na h-Iolaire

450m

Loch Ericht

Continued South East Loch Ericht 2

Loch Ericht 4

955m

400m 450m 500m

550m

Stob an Aonaich Mhoir 855m

Cont'd

Benalder Cottage 1km

791m

There are several plank bridges along the lochside many in poor condition – some missing altogether.

Loch Ericht 4

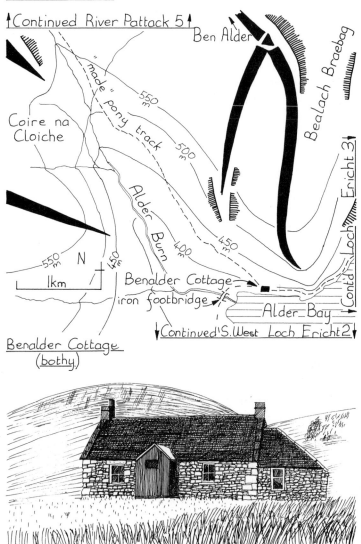

↑Continued River Pattack 5↑

Ben Alder

Bealach Braebag

Coire na Cloiche

"made" pony track

550 m

500 m

450

Alder Burn

400 m

550 m

450 m

N

1km

Contd. Loch Ericht 3↑

Benalder Cottage

iron footbridge →

Alder Bay →

↓Continued S.West Loch Ericht 2↓

Benalder Cottage (bothy.)

76

The environs of Dalnaspidal

Loch Garry always looks wild and inviting from the A9. Access is gained from the Dalnaspidal turning to a route that eventually leads to the shore of Loch Rannoch at Craiganour Lodge. This is a comparatively short through route which feels far more remote than it is. Also included is a stretch of closed 'old A9' and the very rough track into Coire Dhomhain. Note the disused railway station at Dalnaspidal; how could such an elaborate station ever have been justified here?

↑Continued Loch Garry 2↑

old railway station

old A9

A9

gated crossing

gate

Dalnaspidal Lodge
sluice dam

R Garry

long plank bridge

↓Continued Loch Garry 3↓

The old station

Loch Garry 2

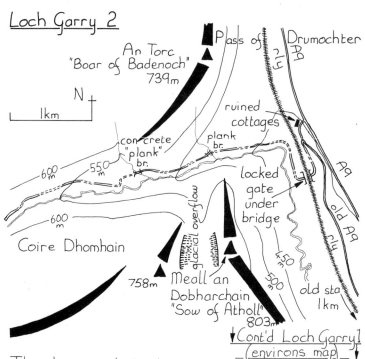

An Torc
"Boar of Badenoch"
739m

Pass of Drumochter

N

1km

con-crete
"plank"
br.

plank
br.

ruined
cottages

600 m

550 m

locked
gate
under
bridge

600 m

Coire Dhomhain

glacial overflow

758m

Meall an
Dobharchain
"Sow of Atholl"
803m

A9

old A9

450 m

500 m

old sta
1km

↓Cont'd Loch Garry 1
(environs map)↓

The above rough track passes between two prominent but not very high mountains affectionately known as "The Sow of Atholl" and "The Boar of Badenoch". Apart from gaining access to some "Munro's" S.E. of Loch Ericht the track has little use for the visitor although it is an ideal way to rid oneself of any surplus energy after a rather short return trip up Loch Garry!!

If we cannot be bothered (or pay!) to plough the many lumps of 'old road' back into the ground then better use should be made of them as cycleway, byroad or whatever. Their abandonment creates an environmentally scarring monument to what is laughingly called 'progress' in our car-bound society.

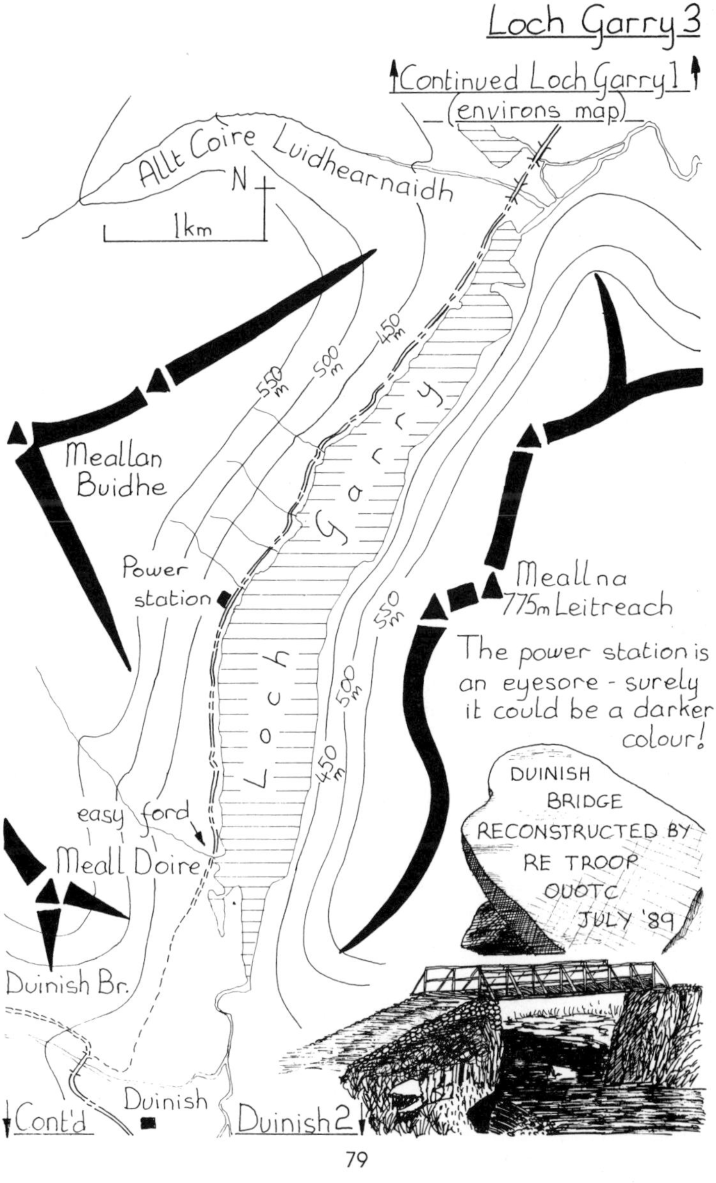

↑Continued Loch Garry 1↑
(environs map)

Allt Coire Luidhearnaidh

N

1km

550m 500m 450m

Meallan
Buidhe

Power
station

Loch Garry

450m

550m

450m 500m

Meall na
775m Leitreach

The power station is
an eyesore - surely
it could be a darker
colour!

easy ford

Meall Doire

Duinish Br.

DUINISH
BRIDGE
RECONSTRUCTED BY
RE TROOP
OUOTC
JULY '89

↑Cont'd   Duinish   Duinish 2↓

Loch Errochty 1

Loch Errochty, which feeds Errochty Water via a Hydro-Electric dam, provides three separate routes, two of which can be linked together by a walk around the pathless head of the loch – though the going is difficult underfoot and navigation around the inlets of the shoreline is time consuming. Your hard-working author surveyed this area on two of the coldest days imaginable.

After camping out in Strathardle in -14°C the temperature rose to a maximum of -5°C! The tracks and loch were sheet ice and visibility was down to 50m. The silence was eerie. Breath froze instantly. Bike brakes froze. Trinafour was gripped by a white frost for days – superb!!

N

Loch Con

1km

450 m

450 m

500 m

Sron Chon 566m

450 m

400 m

ford

L o c h

plk. br.

350 m

Ruighe nan Saorach
(roofed ruin)

450 m

500 m

footbridge
and ford

indistinct hill paths to
Dunalastair Water

opposite

Continued

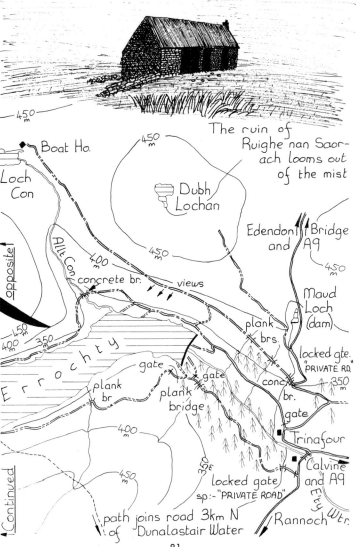

The ruin of Ruighe nan Saorach looms out of the mist

Boat Ho.

Loch Con

Dubh Lochan

450 m

450 m

450 m

Allt Con

400 m

concrete br.

views

Edendon Bridge and A9

450 m

Maud Loch (dam)

450 m

400 m

350 m

plank brs.

locked gte. "PRIVATE RD."

E r r o c h t y

gate

gate

conc. br.

350 m

opposite!

plank br

plank bridge

gate

Trinafour

400 m

350 m

locked gate
sp:- "PRIVATE ROAD"

Calvine and A9

Etty Wtr.

450 m

Continued

path joins road 3km N of Dunalastair Water

Rannoch

Rannoch

Rannoch

Access:- As this section covers the very heart of Rannoch Moor access to the region is divided. To the west the main road over the moor provides access to Loch Ba and Black Corries. The remainder of the routes are accessible from the road to Rannoch Station which runs east to Kinloch Rannoch and the A9. Running north-south between the above roads is the railway which may be used to great advantage in conjunction with one-way through routes. Refer to Rannoch area map.

Accommodation:- Sparse! Kingshouse Hotel (with adjacent camping), the Rannoch Hotel, and the Youth Hostel (nearly always booked up) and bunk-house at Corrour serve the central region. A wider variety of accommodation presents itself as one travels east to Kinloch Rannoch, north to Glencoe or south to Bridge of Orchy, much of which is closed in winter. Self-sufficiency is the key to enjoying the longer through routes.

Geographical Features:- The flat moorland of central Rannoch Moor is surrounded by wild mountains and lochs and numerous lochans and bogs are to be found across the moor. The Glencoe and Black Mount hills form an abrupt western border whilst to the east the land drops to form the main glen enclosing Loch Rannoch, north and south of which are the minor glens featured in this section.

Mountains:- The finest mountain form in this area is surely Buachaille Etive Mor (affectionately known as "The Buckle"), seen at its best in morning light from the Black Corries Lodge track. Carn Gorm and Garbh Meall lie south of Loch Rannoch, less well known and unremarkable "Munros" accessible from Rannoch Forest and Finnart routes. Carn Mairg and the striking outline of Schiehallion watch over the east end of Loch Rannoch.

A fine ridge walk culminating in Carn Dearg and Meall a Bhealaich lies above the Rannoch to Corrour path whilst South West Loch Ericht provides access to the Ben Alder group and Aonach Beag.

Rivers:- The Gaur, which in true Scottish tradition becomes the River Tummel, drains most of the region and eventually joins the Tay. The west of the area is drained by the River Etive in the north and the River Orchy in the south, both of which end up in Loch Etive despite the tortuous route taken by the River Orchy via Loch Awe and the River Awe.

Forests:- The west of the region can only boast a handful of small plantations around Loch Tulla, Ba Cottage and Black Corries. The serious forests start with Gleann Chomraidh as one travels east. This vast commercial forest forms the western section of Rannoch Forest. North of Loch Rannoch are more commercial plantations, a considerable proportion of which are new and unmapped at the time of writing. The star of the show is of course the Black Wood of Rannoch, a fine remnant of the great Caledonian Pine Forest. Also alongside Loch Rannoch are some natural birchwoods - beautiful in late autumn.

Lochs:- Loch Ericht is mentioned under 'West of Drumochter'. Loch Rannoch dominates the region and Loch Ba, Loch Laidon, Loch Eigheach and Loch Ericht all drain into it. Loch Tulla serves as a collection point for water flowing south. Only Lochs Ericht and Eigheach are dammed, which leaves the rest as nature intended.

Emergency:- The longer routes are committing and a sharp eye must be kept on the weather. Black Corries to Loch Laidon is a serious route as is the continuation of Gleann Chomraidh to Loch Tulla. There is a public 'phone at Rannoch Station and Morgan's Den at Corrour. Elsewhere it's up to you! Leave word of your route and keep to the tracks and paths when on the Moor.

Rannoch Routes 1

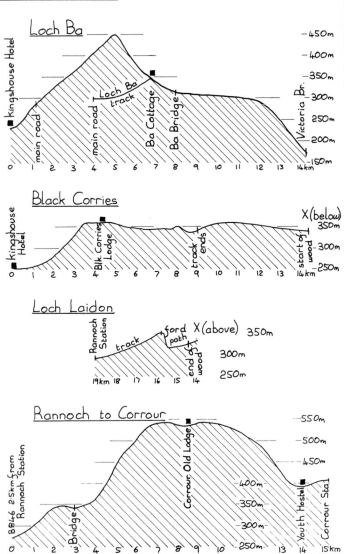

Loch Ba

Kingshouse Hotel — main road — main road — Loch Ba track — Ba Cottage — Ba Bridge — Victoria Br.

450m, 400m, 350m, 300m, 250m, 200m, 150m

0 1 2 3 4 5 6 7 8 9 10 11 12 13 14km

Black Corries

Kingshouse Hotel — Blk. Corries Lodge — track ends — start of wood — X(below)

350m, 300m, 250m

0 1 2 3 4 5 6 7 8 9 10 11 12 13 14km

Loch Laidon

Rannoch Station — track — ford — path — X(above) 350m — end of wood — 300m — 250m

19km 18 17 16 15 14

Rannoch to Corrour

B846 2·5km from Rannoch Station — Bridge — Corrour Old Lodge — Youth Hostel — Corrour Sta.

550m, 500m, 450m, 400m, 350m, 300m, 250m

0 1 2 3 4 5 6 7 8 9 10 11 12 13 14 15km

86

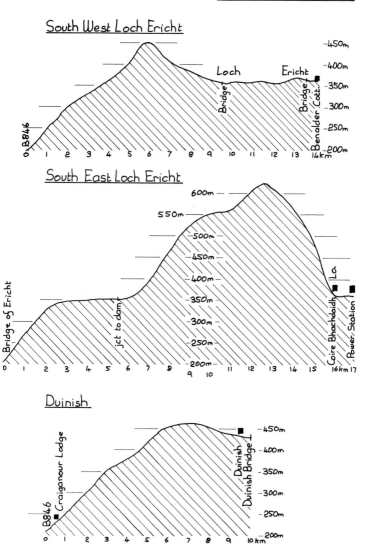

South West Loch Ericht

South East Loch Ericht

Duinish

Rannoch Routes 3

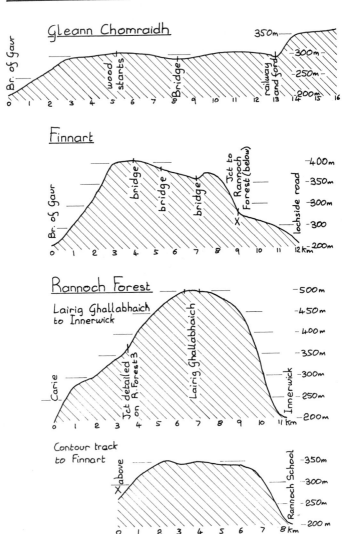

Gleann Chomraidh

Br. of Gaur · wood starts · Bridge · railway and ford

0 1 2 3 4 5 6 7 8 9 10 11 12 13 14 15 16 km

350m · 300m · 250m · 200m

Finnart

Br. of Gaur · bridge · bridge · bridge · Jct to Rannoch Forest (below) · lochside road

0 1 2 3 4 5 6 7 8 9 10 11 12 km

400m · 350m · 300m · 300 · 200m

Rannoch Forest

Lairig Ghallabhaich to Innerwick

Carie · Jct detailed on R.Forest 3 · Lairig Ghallabhaich · Innerwick

0 1 2 3 4 5 6 7 8 9 10 11 km

500m · 450m · 400m · 350m · 300m · 250m · 200m

Contour track to Finnart

X above · Rannoch School

0 1 2 3 4 5 6 7 8 km

350m · 300m · 250m · 200 m

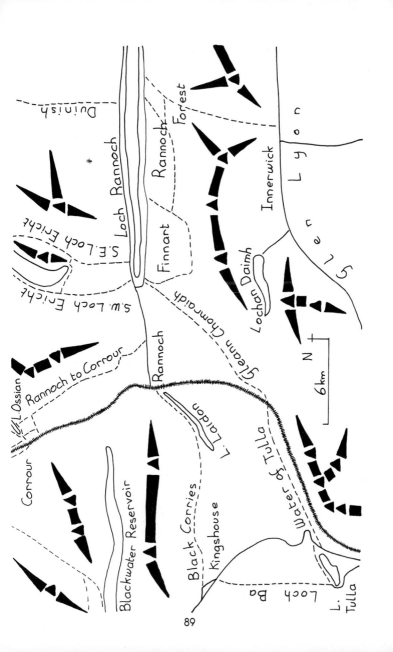

89

Loch Ba 1

Loch Ba covers a section of the West Highland Way from the Kingshouse Hotel to Victoria Bridge at the western end of Loch Tulla. This section of track was, until the building of the 'new' road over Rannoch Moor in the 1930's, the main road north to Fort William, in turn replacing the military road which follows a similar route. The 'A' road connecting Bridge of Orchy to Victoria Bridge is a remnant of the main road. This route has three connections to the A82; via Loch Tulla; a rough track (better down than up!) to Loch Ba; and the third via the ski road near Kingshouse. Here, unfortunately, the characteristic mess associated with skiers' need to park cars within five metres of the bottom of the 'piste' is all too evident. No attempt is made towards landscaping and the car park remains an ugly scar. Although a one-way route, return on the busy road can be avoided by including Victoria Bridge to kingshouse as part of a round trip from Rannoch station via Water of Tulla and returning via Loch Laidon – a committing double crossing of Rannoch Moor:- refer "Link Route 2" at the end of this book. West of Victoria Bridge Glen Kinglass awaits - but that is another story!
Victoria Bridge to Kingshouse is 14km or 9miles and Victoria Bridge to Tulla Cottage is 5km or 3 miles.

Kingshouse Hotel

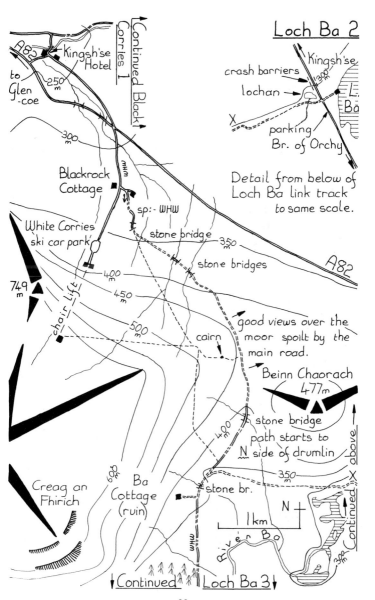

Loch Ba 2

Kingsh'se
crash barriers
lochan →
X
parking
Br. of Orchy
L. Ba

Detail from below of
Loch Ba link track
to same scale.

A82
to Glen-coe
250 m
300 m
Kingsh'se Hotel

Continued Black Corries 1

Blackrock Cottage
WHW
sp:- WHW

White Corries ski car park
stone bridge
350 m
stone bridges
A82

749 m
chair lift
400 m
450 m
500 m
cairn

good views over the moor spoilt by the main road.

Beinn Chaorach 477m

stone bridge
path starts to N side of drumlin
400 m
350 m

Creag an Fhirich
600 m
Ba Cottage (ruin)
WHW
stone br.
River Ba
1 km
N

Continued above X

↓Continued Loch Ba 3↓

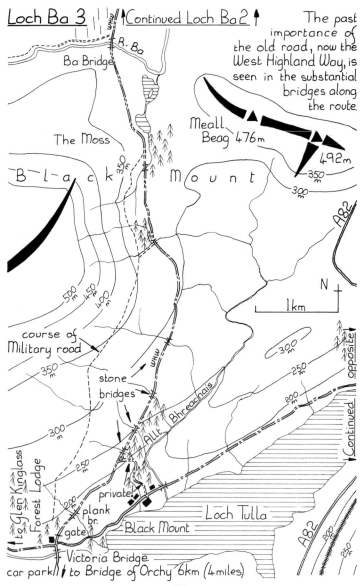

Loch Ba 3

Continued Loch Ba 2 ↑

The past importance of the old road, now the West Highland Way, is seen in the substantial bridges along the route.

R. Ba

Ba Bridge

The Moss

Meall Beag 476m

492m

350m

300m

B l a c k   M o u n t

350m

500m
450m
400m

N

1 km

course of Military road

350m

stone bridges

250m

300m

Allt Bhreacnais

300m

250m

200m

Continued opposite

to Glen Kinglass

Forest Lodge

250m

200m

private!

plank br.

gate

Black Mount

Loch Tulla

A82

200m

250m

car park

Victoria Bridge

to Bridge of Orchy 6km (4 miles)

Ba Bridge

The gate above Victoria Bridge

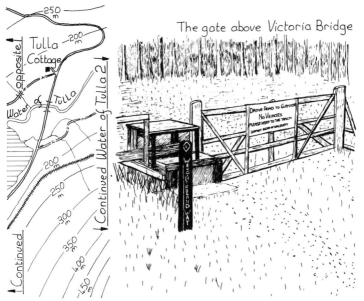

Black Corries 1

The Black Corries track heads straight across Rannoch Moor from Kingshouse Hotel, links up with the Loch Laidon tracks and forms part of "Link route 2". The centre section of the route is not a bike ride due to the extremely rough terrain. The track ends near the Menzie's stone, the significance of which your author has yet to discover. The next 6km or 4miles to the forest tracks of Loch Laidon are slow going indeed. The railway station at Rannoch assists in making the one-way trip. The right of way has been diverted around Black Corries Lodge, the environs of which are private. [I use the word "diverted" loosely as no provision whatsoever had been made at the time of survey and a rough path through heather, streams and bog has to be endured for 250m]

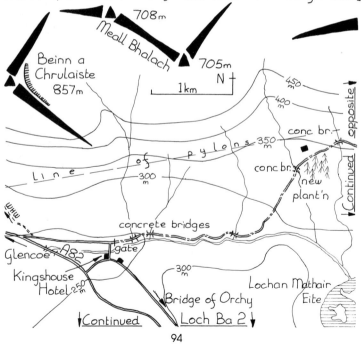

↓Continued

↓Continued opposite

↓Bridge of Orchy
Loch Ba 2↓

Beinn a Chrulaiste 857m

708m

Meall Bhalach

705m

N

1km

450 m

400 m

350 m

conc br.

conc br.

new plant'n

Line of pylons

300 m

WHW

concrete bridges

Glencoe A82

gate

Kingshouse Hotel 250m

300 m

Lochan Mathair Eite

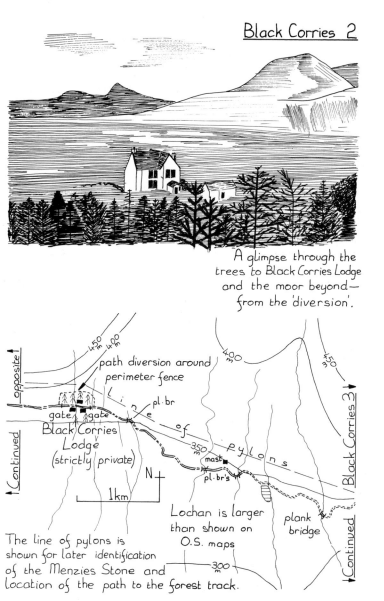

A glimpse through the trees to Black Corries Lodge and the moor beyond— from the 'diversion'.

path diversion around perimeter fence

450 m 400 m

400 m

450 m

opposite↑

Line of Pylons

pl. br

350

mast

pl. br's

gate   gate

Black Corries Lodge (strictly private)

N

1km

Lochan is larger than shown on O.S. maps

plank bridge

The line of pylons is shown for later identification of the Menzies Stone and location of the path to the forest track.

300

←Continued

Black Corries 3→

Continued→

Black Corries 3

Location of the Menzie's Stone

Sketch shows the Menzie's Stone, the "change of direction" pylon used to locate same, with Buachaille Etive Mor and Glencoe in the distance.

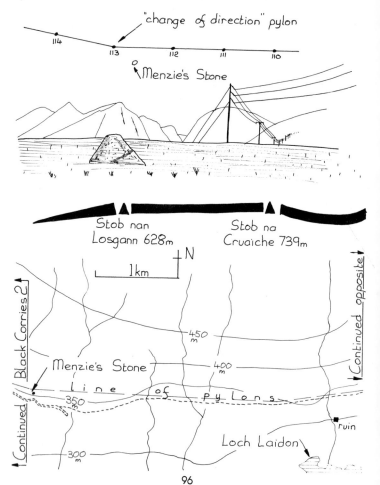

Loch Laidon

This route starts at Rannoch Station - the route is mapped as a continuation of the Black Corries path. Loch Laidon provides either a series of short walks or rides from Rannoch or an extended sortie to the end of the wood. However the main reason for its inclusion is the long walkers' path to Kingshouse.

<u>Note X</u> :- A rough path rises from pylon No 47 to the ford at the end of the forest track. It is <u>NOT</u> possible to continue along the line of pylons due to deer fencing.

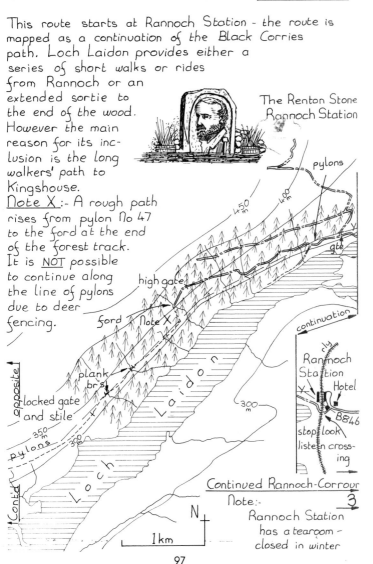

The Renton Stone
Rannoch Station

pylons

gte

high gate

450 m

400 m

ford   Note X

plank br'g

locked gate and stile

opposite

350 m

300

pylons

300 m

300 m

Contd

r
o
d
o
V
o
h
V
o
h

continuation

rly

Rannoch Station   Hotel

B846

stop look listen crossing

Continued Rannoch-Corrour **3**

Note:-
　　Rannoch Station
　　has a tearoom -
　　closed in winter

N

1km

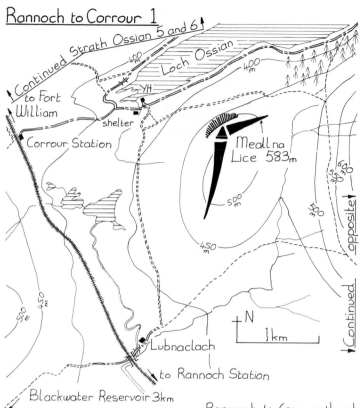

Rannoch to Corrour, though not strictly a "glen" route is of some strategic importance in linking not only two railway stations, and the Rannoch road to Strath Ossian, but the many routes radiating from the two stations. The railway may be used in making a one-way walk or ride, this being a convenient 15km or 9.5 miles. Although not your author's first choice as a bike ride the paths are, in dry weather, possible with a bike and justifiable if part of a longer tour. The drop down to Lubnaclach should be avoided with a bike - the high path providing a far better option despite the track to the Youth Hostel.

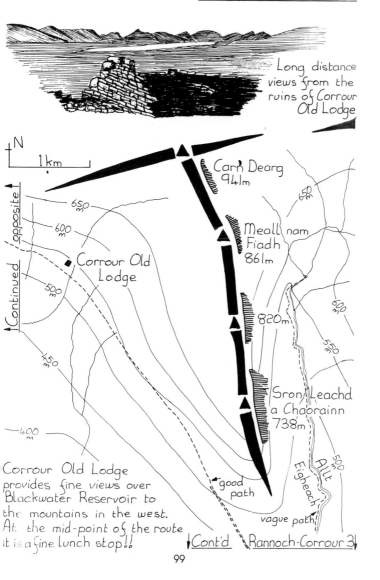

Long distance views from the ruins of Corrour Old Lodge

N

1 km

Continued opposite ↑

650 m
600 m
500 m
450 m
400 m

Carn Dearg 941m

Meall nam Fiadh 861m

820m

Corrour Old Lodge

650 m
600 m
550 m
500 m

Sron Leachd a Chaorainn 738m

good path

Allt Eigheach

vague path

Corrour Old Lodge provides fine views over Blackwater Reservoir to the mountains in the west. At the mid-point of the route it is a fine lunch stop!!

↓Cont'd   Rannoch-Corrour 3↓

Rannoch to Corrour 3

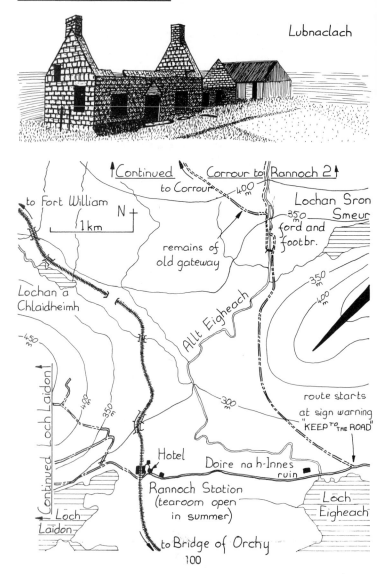

Lubnaclach

↑ Continued to Corrour

Corrour to Rannoch 2 ↑

to Fort William

N ↑

1km

Lochan Sron Smeur

350 m

ford and footbr.

remains of old gateway

400 m

Lochan a Chlaidheimh

Allt Eigheach

350 m

400 m

-450 m

Continued Loch Laidon ↑

400

350

300

route starts at sign warning "KEEP TO THE ROAD"

Hotel

Doire na h-Innes ruin

Loch Eigheach

Rannoch Station (tearoom open in summer)

← Loch Laidon

↓ to Bridge of Orchy

100

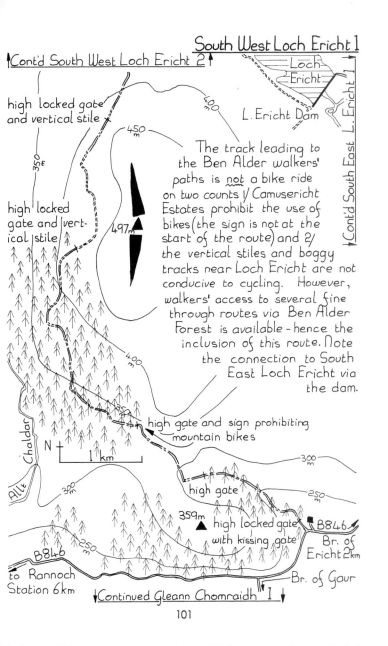

Loch Ericht

↑Cont'd South West Loch Ericht 2↑

L. Ericht Dam

high locked gate
and vertical stile

↑Cont'd South East L. Ericht↑

450 m

400 m

350 m

The track leading to
the Ben Alder walkers'
paths is not a bike ride
on two counts 1/ Camusericht
Estates prohibit the use of
bikes (the sign is not at the
start of the route) and 2/
the vertical stiles and boggy
tracks near Loch Ericht are not
conducive to cycling. However,
walkers' access to several fine
through routes via Ben Alder
Forest is available – hence the
inclusion of this route. Note
the connection to South
East Loch Ericht via
the dam.

high locked
gate and vert-
ical stile

497m

400

250 m

high gate and sign prohibiting
mountain bikes

Allt Chaldar

N

1 km

300 m

300 m

300 m

250 m

250 m

high gate

359m

high locked gate
with kissing gate

B846
Br. of
Ericht 2km

B846
to Rannoch
Station 6km

Br. of Gaur

↓Continued Gleann Chomraidh 1↓

South West Loch Ericht 2

↑ Continued Loch Ericht 4 ↑

The strange timber bridge leading to Benalder Cottage

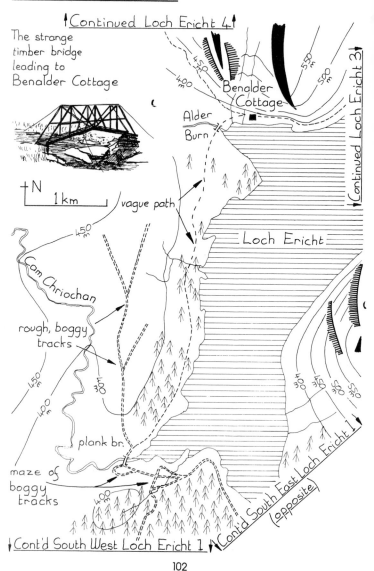

↑N
1 km

Continued Loch Ericht 3

450
400
550
500

Benalder Cottage

Alder Burn

vague path

Loch Ericht

Cam Chriochan

450

rough, boggy tracks

450
400
400
350

plank br.

maze of boggy tracks

400

400
350
300
355
350
350
355

↑ Cont'd South West Loch Ericht 1 ↑

Cont'd South East Loch Ericht 1 (opposite)

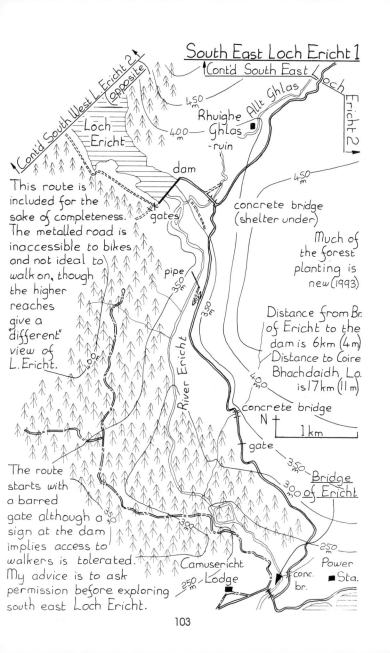

Loch Ericht 2

Cont'd South West L. Ericht 2 (opposite)

450 m

Rhuighe Allt Ghlas
Ghlas
-ruin

Loch
Ericht

400 m

450 m

dam

concrete bridge
(shelter under)

gates

This route is
included for the
sake of completeness.
The metalled road is
inaccessible to bikes
and not ideal to
walk on, though
the higher
reaches
give a
"different"
view of
L. Ericht.

pipe

350 m

350 m

River Ericht

Much of
the forest
planting is
new (1993)

Distance from Br.
of Ericht to the
dam is 6km (4m)
Distance to Coire
Bhachdaidh Lo.
is 17km (11m)

400 m

concrete bridge
N ↑
|— 1 km —|

gate

350 m

300 m

Bridge
of Ericht

The route
starts with
a barred
gate although a
sign at the dam
implies access to
walkers is tolerated.
My advice is to ask
permission before exploring
south east Loch Ericht.

300 m

300 m

250 m

Camusericht
Lodge

250 m

conc.
br.

Power
Sta.

250 m

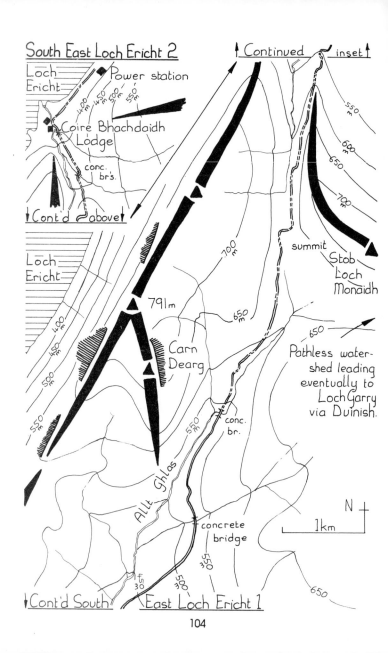

South East Loch Ericht 2

Loch Ericht

Power station

Coire Bhachdaidh Lodge

conc. brs.

↑ Cont'd above ↑

Loch Ericht

791m

Carn Dearg

↑ Continued   inset ↑

summit

Stob Loch Monaidh

Pathless water-shed leading eventually to Loch Garry via Duinish.

conc. br.

Allt Ghlas

concrete bridge

N

1km

↓ Cont'd South   East Loch Ericht 1

The track to Duinish forms one half of a short (17km or 11m) through route from Loch Rannoch to the A9 at Dalnaspidal passing through some remote country between the watershed and the head of Loch Garry. There is shelter at Duinish, an interesting bridge and no major ford. (Refer Loch Garry) The area immediately east of Duinish is remarkably flat and here lies one of two possible cross-country routes to Loch Errochty. Experience in wilderness walking is required for either of these two pathless excursions which are notable for their lack of landmarks, though both follow rivers down to the Loch. A third wilderness route runs west from Duinish to the Loch Ericht power station road, this being a very committing route. An hour should be allowed for each 2-2.5km or 1.5 miles off the tracks, and landowners' permission should be sought. L.Rannoch to L.Garry is 'OK' with a bike apart from a short struggle north of Duinish Bridge.

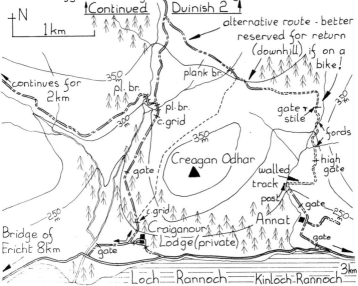

+N
1km

Continued   Duinish 2

alternative route - better
reserved for return
(downhill) if on a
bike!

plank br

continues for
2km

350
pl. br.

300

pl. br.
c.grid

350

gate
stile

350

fords

high
gate

Creagan Odhar

walled
track

post

Annat

gate

gate

250

gate

c.grid

Craiganour
Lodge (private)

Bridge of
Ericht 8km

gate

Loch Rannoch Kinloch-Rannoch

3km

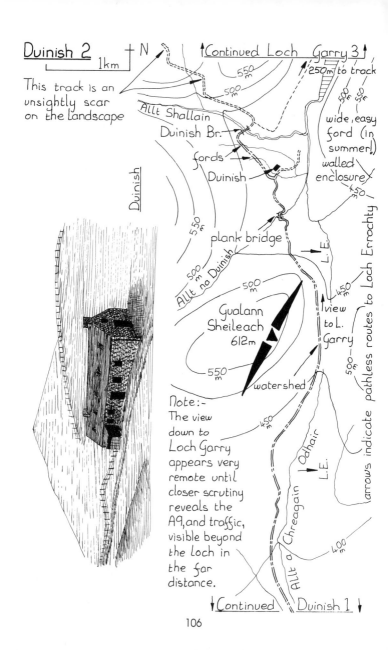

1km

↑ Continued Loch Garry 3 ↑

This track is an
unsightly scar
on the landscape

550
500
250m to track

Allt Shallain

Duinish Br.

500 · 550

wide, easy
ford (in
summer!)

fords

walled
enclosure

Duinish

450 · 350

Duinish

plank bridge

L.E.

Allt na Duinish

500m

550m

500
m

Gualann
Sheileach
612m

view
to L.
Garry

450

550
m

watershed

500
m

450

arrows indicate pathless routes to Loch Errochty

Note:-
The view
down to
Loch Garry
appears very
remote until
closer scrutiny
reveals the
A9, and traffic,
visible beyond
the Loch in
the far
distance.

Allt a Odhair

L.E.

Allt a Chreagain

400
m

↓ Continued Duinish 1 ↓

Gleann Chomraidh 1

Gleann Chomraidh and the western section of Rannoch Forest was surveyed by yours truly in the mist and rain of Christmas 1992 - no report on the views! It explores the planted forests and the connection through to Water of Tulla - for walkers only. The continuation of the track beyond the railway was not included in my survey as the track shares a railway bridge with a river, which was not only full but had an inch of ice on it! As a through walk to Bridge of Orchy (30km or 19miles) or an excursion to the railway only (13km or 8miles one way). Gleann Chomraidh provides a glimpse of some of the wildest moorland in Britain, especially if your trip, as mine, is undertaken in mist and pouring rain!

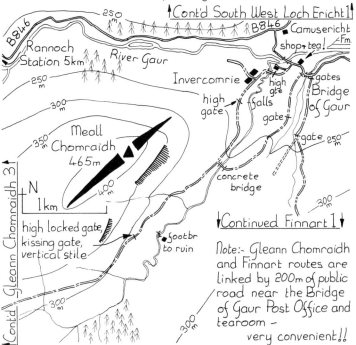

↑Cont'd South West Loch Ericht 1↑

250 m

B846

B846 Camusericht

shop + tea!

Fm.

Rannoch Station 5km

River Gaur

Invercomrie

high gate

Bridge of Gaur

250 m

300 m

high gate

falls

gate

gates

high gate

Meall Chomraidh 465m

350 m

400 m

gate 250 m

concrete bridge

N

1 km

300 m

high locked gate, kissing gate, vertical stile

footbr to ruin

↓Continued Finnart 1↓

Note:- Gleann Chomraidh and Finnart routes are linked by 200m of public road near the Bridge of Gaur Post Office and tearoom -
very convenient!!

300 m

300 m

←Cont'd Gleann Chomraidh 3→

Gleann Chomraidh 2

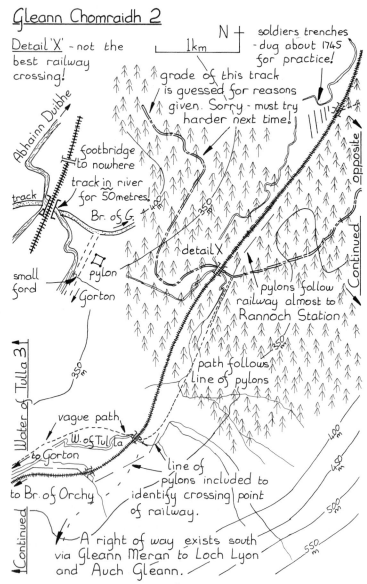

Detail 'X' – not the best railway crossing!

N

1km

soldiers trenches – dug about 1745 for practice!

grade of this track is guessed for reasons given. Sorry – must try harder next time!

Abhainn Duibhe

footbridge to nowhere

track in river for 50 metres!

Br. of G.

track

400 m

350 m

detail X

Continued opposite

small ford

pylon

Gorton

pylons follow railway almost to Rannoch Station

Water of Tulla 3

350 m

350 m

path follows line of pylons

vague path

W. of Tulla

to Gorton

400 m

450 m

line of pylons included to identify crossing point of railway.

to Br. of Orchy

500 m

550 m

Continued

A right of way exists south via Gleann Meran to Loch Lyon and Auch Gleann.

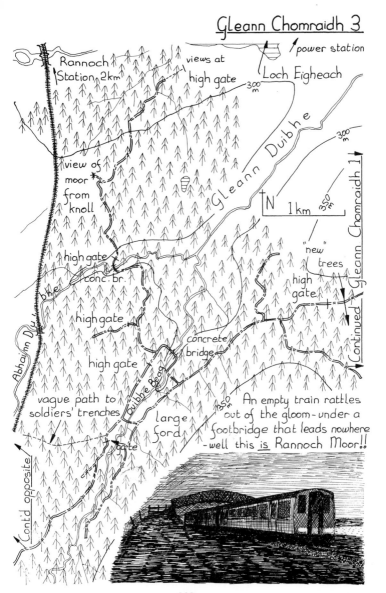

power station

Loch Eigheach

Rannoch Station 2km

views at high gate

300 m

Gleann Duibhe

300 m

view of moor from knoll

N 1km

350 m

high gate

conc. br.

"new" trees

high gate

Abhainn Duibhe

high gate

high gate

concrete bridge

Continued Gleann Chomraidh 1

Duibhe Beag

vague path to soldiers' trenches

large ford

gate

350 m

Contd opposite

An empty train rattles out of the gloom - under a footbridge that leads nowhere - well this *is* Rannoch Moor!!

109

Finnart 1

The Finnart tracks, starting from Bridge of Gaur provide a steep climb to a flat upper sanctuary which is surrounded by high mountains yet only 3km from the start of the route. An excellent descending track then runs down to the western access to the eastern section of Rannoch Forest which can then be explored. The above direction of travel takes advantage of the best views over Loch Rannoch on the descent to the woods. The continuing descent emerges on a farm road leading to the public road along the south side of Loch Rannoch. Bridge of Gaur to the start of the wood is 10km or 6m, keeping to the track, or 12km (8m) down to the road, some 5km (3m) from Bridge of Gaur. There is no shelter en route - so if it rains - tough!

↑Continued South West Loch Ericht 1↑

Continued Gleann Chomraidh 1

B846 Br. of Gaur   Finnart

R. Gaur

shop + tea

gate - s.p. Finnart Estate

N

1km

gate   250m

gate   300m
        350m

stone bridge

400m

450m

opposite

400m

gate and c. grid Luban Feith a Mhadaidh

gate

high locked gate

girder
• conc. br.

450m

girder
+ conc. br.

Meall an Stalcair
512m

400m

450m

←Continued

Allt Easan Stalcair

500m

500m

657m

Allt Sloc na Creadha

110

Finnart Lo.

Loch Rannoch

250 m

350 m

Coille Mhor

Loch Finnart

gate

gte.

300 m

Loch Monaghan

gates

250 m

pair of gates

conc. br.

ravine

gate

Cnoc Eoghainn

300

350 m

300

conc. br.

400 m

450 m

high gate

opposite

601 m

Leagag

views

high locked
gate and
kissing gate

pair of gates

350

350

Scots Pine
- but 50%
dead - no
saplings

400 m

450 m

Cross
Craigs
747m

Meall a
Bhobuir
655m

Continued

Continued

Rannoch Forest 3

Continued

N

1 km

500 m

111

Rannoch Forest 1

Rannoch Forest comprises a large area of both natural and planted forest alongside the south shore of Loch Rannoch. The natural Scots Pine woodland, Black Wood of Rannoch, contains the finest examples of Scots Pine outside the Rothiemurchus and Abernethy Forests (east of Aviemore in the Cairngorms) This remnant of the original Caledonian Pine Forest is a living monument to the natural pine forests that once clothed much of Scotland. Many remaining examples of Scots Pine are as those depicted on map 'Finnart 2', subject to browsing by the too-high deer population which prevents re-generation of trees. The Black Wood of Rannoch is therefore a sacred place; to stand among the old giants of the forest is to experience a piece of living history.... Rannoch School lies in the centre of the woods and is best avoided. Your author encountered a reluctant group of cross-country runners on his travels – what a place to go to school – I hope the pupils appreciate it!

The many forest tracks extend up to the Lairig Ghallabhaich which connects Rannoch Forest to Glen Lyon at Innerwick, a distance of about 12-13km depending on the route taken down to Loch Rannoch. There is no shelter but one is never very far from the road-apart from the exposed Lairig Ghallabhaich.

Innerwick
War Memorial

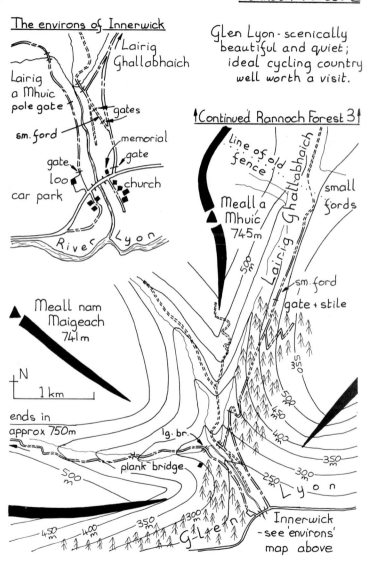

The environs of Innerwick

Lairig
Ghallabhaich

Lairig
a Mhuic
pole gate

gates

sm. ford

memorial
gate

gate
loo
car park

church

River Lyon

Glen Lyon - scenically
beautiful and quiet;
ideal cycling country
well worth a visit.

↑Continued Rannoch Forest 3↑

line of old
fence

small
fords

Meall a
Mhuic
745m

Lairig-Ghallabhaich

500 m

sm. ford
gate + stile

▲ Meall nam
Maigeach
741m

550 m

N
1 km

500 m
450 m
400 m

ends in
approx 750m

350 m

lg. br.

plank bridge

500
m

300 m
250 m

L y o n

450 m
400 m

350 m
300 m

Innerwick
- see 'environs'
map above

G l e n

113

Rannoch Forest 3

It is obviously possible to plan your route avoiding intrusion into the environs of Rannoch School.

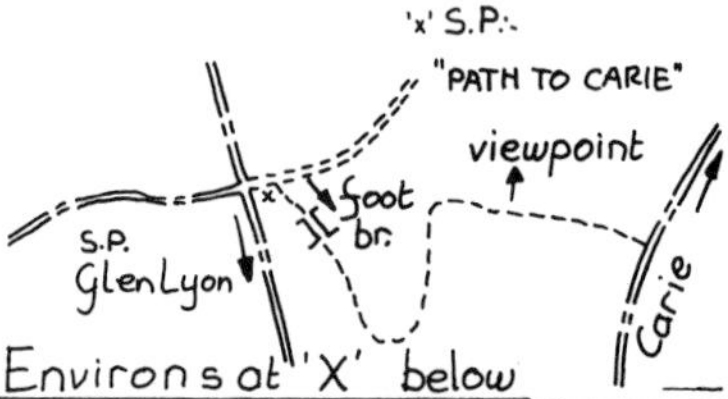

'x' S.P.
"PATH TO CARIE"
viewpoint
S.P. Glen Lyon
foot br.
Carie
Environs at 'x' below

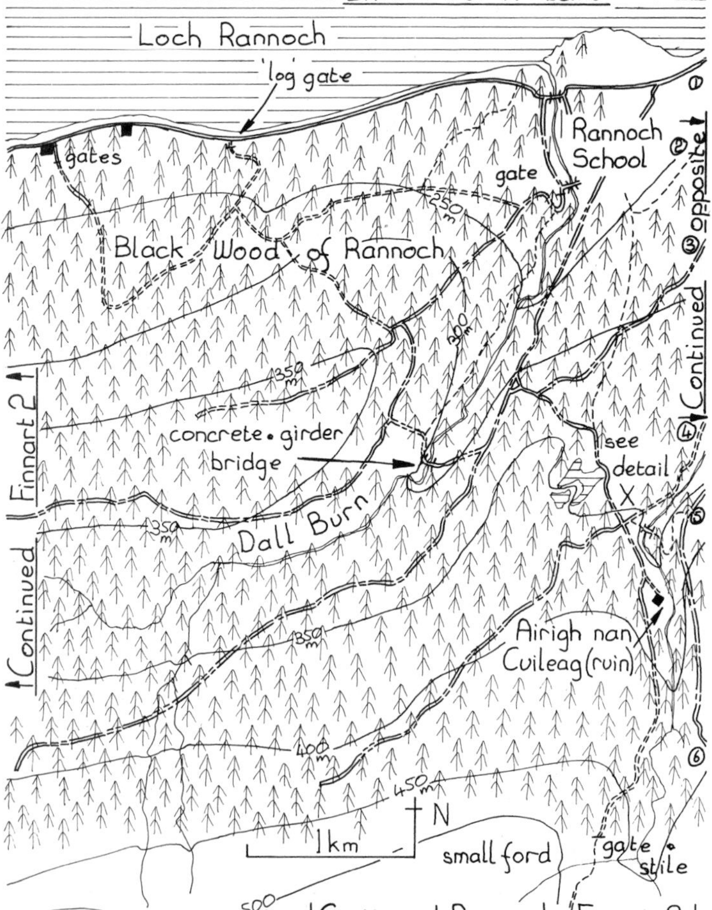

Loch Rannoch

'log gate

gates

Rannoch School

gate

Black Wood of Rannoch

350 m

concrete girder bridge

Finnart 2

see detail

X

Continued

Dall Burn

350 m

Airigh nan Cuileag (ruin)

Continued

400 m

450 m

1 km

N

small ford

gate
stile

500 m

↓Continued Rannoch Forest 2↓

114

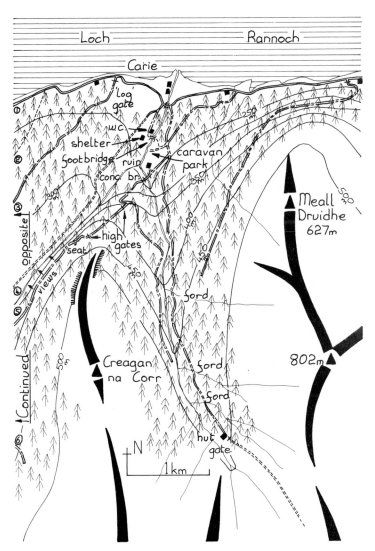

Orchy to Killin

Orchy to Killin

Access:- The Orchy to Killin area lies north of the only main road running east to west, yet immediately south of Rannoch Moor, though this area is not strictly Rannoch, either in location or geographically. The A82 road runs from Crianlarich up the western side before crossing the Moor and the A85 Crianlarich/Killin/Aberfeldy road forms the south east border. The B846 links this to the Rannoch road between Aberfeldy and Tummel Bridge. Minor roads run up Glens Lochay and Lyon. The railway serves Crianlarich, Tyndrum and Bridge of Orchy in the west.

Accommodation:- A sprinkling of accommodation is available along the above-mentioned main roads only. Very little is available elsewhere. There are campsites at Tyndrum, Glen Dochart, Killin, Loch Tay and Kenmore. Youth Hostels are to be found at Crianlarich and Killin. Killin is the main tourist centre with Tyndrum and Kenmore providing an ever-increasing variety of accommodation. Tourist information centres are at Tyndrum and Killin, both closed in winter, and also at Aberfeldy. [It is your author's humble opinion that the Scottish tourist industry does itself a dis-service by shutting down too early - often before English October half term holiday, and re-opening too late - sometimes after Easter. Scotland is beautiful in winter - more winter accommodation please!]

Geographical Features:- An area of east to west glens separated by high mountains. These glens are particularly scenic partly due to the main glens not being very high above sea level - in contrast to the wild glens further north - the green vegetation providing a change from moorland heather.

Mountains:- Ben Lawers is the highest by far and with its visitor centre and proximity to Killin, and a road half way up, is deservedly popular with walkers. Your author will reserve judgement on the principle of inflicting a "visitor centre" on a mountain. Mountains stand high, proud, aloof. A visitor centre reduces its status from "sacred" to "theme park" and produces an ugly, eroded tourist path. An extreme view? Perhaps. West of Lawers are many grand heights, readily accessible from Glen Lyon and Glen Lochay. The finest mountain region lies east of the Crianlarich to Bridge of Orchy road and railway, where a number of wilder, more remote thousand-metre peaks await the walker.

Rivers:— Apart from Auch Gleann and Water of Tulla which drain into the west-flowing River Orchy, every other river in the region finds its way into the Tay, even, some which rise west of Tyndrum. With the notable exceptions of Water of Tulla and especially Auch Gleann, fords do not feature in the following routes.

Forests:— Drummond Hill is the only route based on forest tracks. Other plantations, mostly in Glen Lyon, are fairly small. Much of the beauty of the region lies in the natural woods of the glens - in this the lower reaches of Glen Lyon and Glen Lochay excel, spoilt only by being interspersed by square-edged patches of new planting; if only it was viable to plant new forests with uneven, natural edges!

Lochs:— Loch an Daimh and Loch Lyon, both hydro-electric dams, provide wild stretches of water reaching into the heart of the mountains. Lochan na Lairig also deserves mention, lying behind an ugly dam at the side of the Ben Lawers road, the crags behind it forming an impressive backdrop. Loch Tay, best enjoyed by cycling along its quiet, south side, obviously dominates the region. Free of dams, each end of the loch is a tourist "honeypot" centred around Killin and the watersports at Kenmore.

Emergency:— Routes are generally short and populated so just shout "help!" The exception is Auch Gleann where the fords demand respect and the through route to Loch Lyon is remote - this is a serious mountain area. Public phones are scarce, rely on occupied houses.

Orchy to Killin Routes 1

Water of Tulla

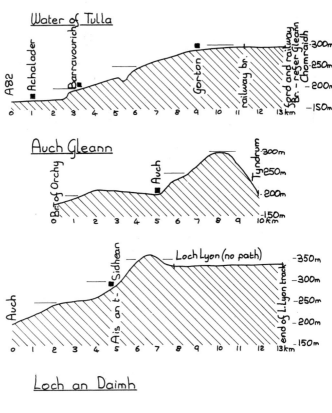

Achalader · A82 · Barravourich · Gorton · railway bn. · Sgrd and railway · Br. - reser Gleann Chomraidh

300m / 250m / 200m / 150m

0 1 2 3 4 5 6 7 8 9 10 11 12 13km

Auch Gleann

Br of Orchy · Auch · Tyndrum

300m / 250m / 200m / 150m

0 1 2 3 4 5 6 7 8 9 10km

Auch · Ais an t- Sidhean · Loch Lyon (no path) · end of L.Lyon track

350m / 300m / 250m / 200m / 150m

0 1 2 3 4 5 6 7 8 9 10 11 12 13km

Loch an Daimh

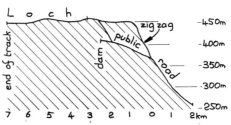

L o c h · end of track · dam · public · zig zag · road

450m / 400m / 350m / 300m / 250m

7 6 5 4 3 2 1 0 1 2km

Loch Lyon

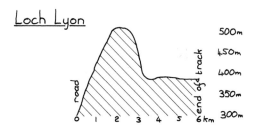

Glen Lochay.

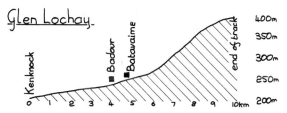

low level track shown - the high track contours at 400m

Auchlyne West Burn

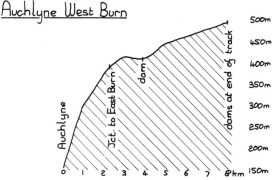

Drummond Hill

No specific route can be given but a considerable amount of easily-graded climbing exists between 120m and about 400m above sea level.

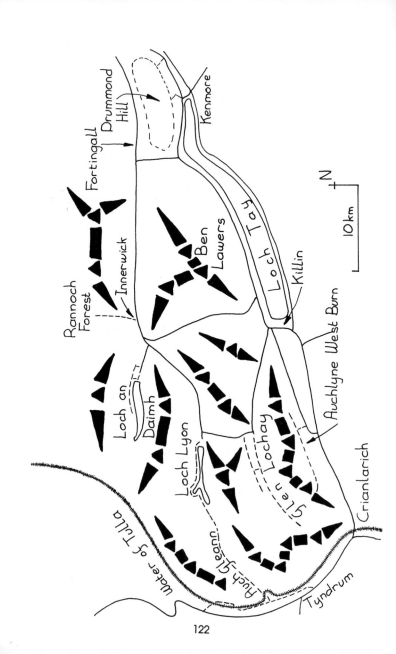

The Water of Tulla track runs from Loch Tulla to Gorton Bothy, rising only 130m in height in its entire length. Beyond the bothy a rough and indistinct path crosses the railway line and follows a line of pylons to join the forest tracks leading to Gleann Chomraidh and Bridge of Gaur. The centre section of the through route, from Gorton to "detail X" on Gleann Chomraidh 2 is not suitable for cyclists though the return trip to Gorton is ideal. There are two large fords at the start of the route (wide but usually not too deep) and cattle are to be encountered throughout the route (including large bull!). The distance, one way from Water of Tulla to Gorton is 9km (6miles); to "detail X" in Gleann Chomraidh is 15km or 9miles;

Barravourich

and to Bridge of Gaur is 27km or 17miles. Add 3km or 2 miles to the above distances from Bridge of Orchy. The only shelter available is at Gorton.

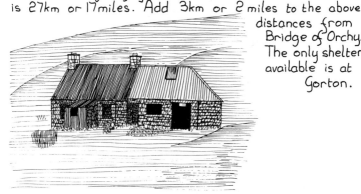

<u>Gorton Bothy</u>

Water of Tulla 2

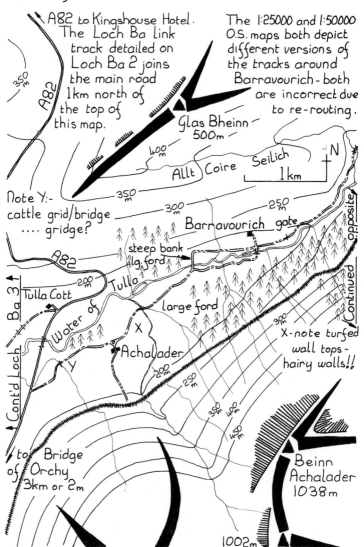

A82 to Kingshouse Hotel.
The Loch Ba Link track detailed on Loch Ba 2 joins the main road 1km north of the top of this map.

The 1:25000 and 1:50000 O.S. maps both depict different versions of the tracks around Barravourich - both are incorrect due to re-routing.

Glas Bheinn
500m

350m

400m

A82

Allt Coire Seilich

N

1km

Note Y:-
cattle grid/bridge
.... gridge?

350m

300m

250m

Barravourich gate

steep bank
lg. ford

A82

200m

Tulla Cott

Water of Tulla

large ford

X

Achalader

200m

250m

300m

X - note turfed wall tops - hairy walls!!

Y

Cont'd Loch Ba 3

to Bridge of Orchy
3km or 2m

300m
400m
450m

Beinn Achalader
1038m

1002m

Continued opposite

124

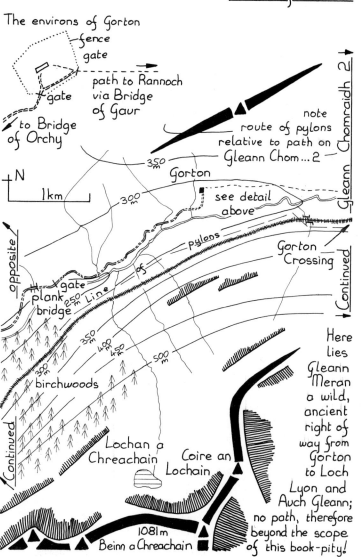

The environs of Gorton

fence

gate

path to Rannoch via Bridge of Gaur

gate

to Bridge of Orchy

Gleann Chomraidh 2

note route of pylons relative to path on Gleann Chom...2

350 m

N

1km

300 m

Gorton

see detail above

opposite

pylons

Gorton Crossing

gate

plank bridge

250 m

Line

of

Continued

350 m

400 m

450 m

500 m

300 m

birchwoods

Continued

Here lies Gleann Meran a wild, ancient right of way from Gorton to Loch Lyon and Auch Gleann; no path, therefore beyond the scope of this book-pity!

Lochan a Chreachain

Coire an Lochain

1081m

Beinn a Chreachain

Auch Gleann 1

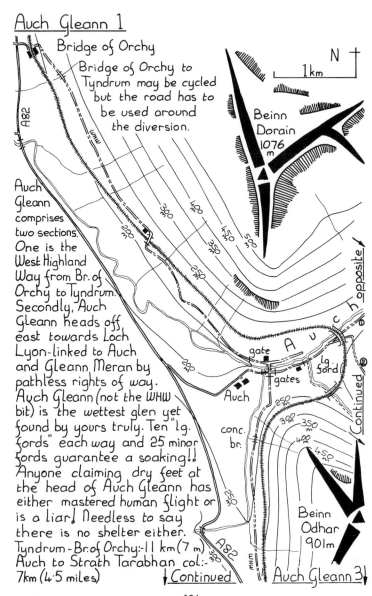

Bridge of Orchy

Bridge of Orchy to Tyndrum may be cycled but the road has to be used around the diversion.

Beinn Dorain 1076 m

Auch Gleann comprises two sections. One is the West Highland Way from Br. of Orchy to Tyndrum. Secondly, Auch Gleann heads off east towards Loch Lyon-linked to Auch and Gleann Meran by pathless rights of way. Auch Gleann (not the WHW bit) is the wettest glen yet found by yours truly. Ten "lg. fords" each way and 25 minor fords guarantee a soaking!! Anyone claiming dry feet at the head of Auch Gleann has either mastered human flight or is a liar! Needless to say there is no shelter either. Tyndrum-Br. of Orchy:-11 km (7 m) Auch to Strath Tarabhan col:- 7km (4·5 miles)

N

1 km

A82

WHW

400
350
300
250
200
450
500

Auch

Auch

gate
gates
lg. ford

conc. br.

250
300
350
400
450

Beinn Odhar 901m

Continued opposite

↓ Continued

Auch Gleann 3↓

A82

WHW

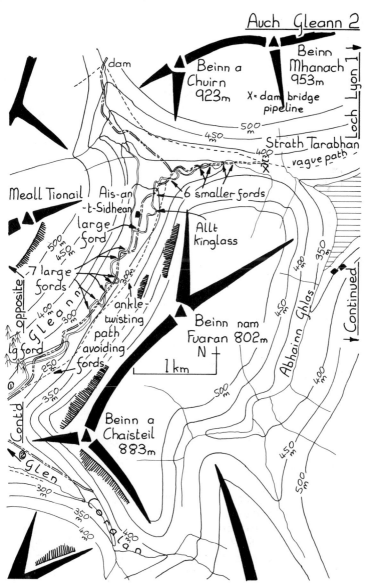

Beinn a Chuirn 923m

Beinn Mhanach 953m

X = dam bridge pipeline

Loch Lyon 1

dam

500 m

450

400

Strath Tarabhan

vague path

X

Meall Tionail

Ais-an-t-Sidhean

6 smaller fords

large ford

Allt kinglass

500 m

450

7 large fords

400

300

opposite

Gleann

ankle-twisting path avoiding fords

lg ford

250

Beinn nam Fuaran 802m

N

350

400

450

Abhainn Ghlas

Continued

350

400

1 km

500

Contd

350

Beinn a Chaisteil 883m

450

500

Glen Cor Glan

300 m

350 m

400

400

450

500

127

Auch Gleann 3

↑ Continued Auch Gleann 1 ↑

This section follows the route of the old road north of Tyndrum which eventually continued north past Ba Cottage — see Loch Ba. It is good to see an old road put to use as the West Highland Way giving enjoyment to many despite the ever present traffic noise -an unwelcome feature of the W.H.W. The footpath diversion X-Y is around a missing bridge and has created an ugly scar due to erosion. A new footbridge is needed. Cyclists can avoid this section by following the busy road from Y to Z.

The viaduct

Loch an Daimh (or Daimph) is a shorter route than would normally qualify for inclusion but the beauty of the scenery, including the public road section from Glen Lyon, more than justifies the departure from longer routes. As an evening or half-day walk or a side-trip to a bike ride along Glen Lyon, Loch an Daimh is well worth seeking out.

Note:- free range cows on track!

N ↑

1 km

500 to Glen Lyon road

gate

Allt Conait

450

550

500

550

450

400

350

conc. brs.

end of public road

pole gate

plank bridge

pl. brs.

Loch an Daimh

footbridge
ford

550
500

450 500 550

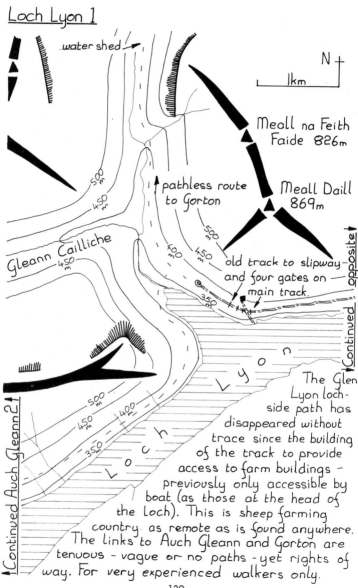

water shed

N

1km

Meall na Feith Faide 826m

Meall Daill 869m

pathless route to Gorton

Gleann Cailliche

500m
450m
450m

500m
450m
400m
350m

old track to slipway and four gates on main track.

Continued opposite

The Glen Lyon loch-side path has disappeared without trace since the building of the track to provide access to farm buildings — previously only accessible by boat (as those at the head of the loch). This is sheep farming country as remote as is found anywhere. The links to Auch Gleann and Gorton are tenuous — vague or no paths — yet rights of way. For very experienced walkers only.

Loch Lyon

500m
450m
400m
350m

Continued Auch Gleann 21

130

The road from Loch Lyon dam to Glen Lochay is shown on the 1993 O.S. map as a track. The surfaced road is not publicised as Glen Lyon and Glen Lochay are signposted as no through roads - so don't tell anyone!

Distance from the gates at the start 'X' to the end of the track is 6km (4m). A pathless 11km (7m) continues to Gorton at 17km (10.5m) and a pathless 7km (4.5m) continues to meet the Auch Gleann track.

Total distances to:-
1/ Br. of Gaur 29km (18m)
2/ Rd. at Auch 21km (13m)
3/ Road at Achallader 25km (16m)

796m

N

1 km

waterfall below plank bridge

opp. site!

line of old path

gate

gate

500

400

350

gates

R. Lyon

L o c h   L y o n

this bit of road is pop-ulated by tons of prime Highland beef, including a large bull!

Continued

400 m

450

500 m

Meall a Chall 756m

450 m

500 m

to Glen Lochay

Bad Donn 720m

131

Glen Lochay 1

The Glen Lochay tracks comprise a low level route thro' farmland and a high level route which serves the Loch an Daimh hydro scheme, as does the pipe across Glen Lochay from Auchlyne West Burn. New tracks at the head of the glen and linking high and low level routes extend the possibilities for exploration.

ford • dam

dam

gate 300

Badour

500 m

400 m

250

350 m

Batavaime

ford

Sail Dubh

footbridge
dam • ford

gates
250

footbridges

300 350 400 450

500

ford, footbridge
and 2 gates

Continued opposite

dams

small
fords

+N

1km

w'fall

Meall
Glas 957m

small
fords

500 m 450 m 400 m

400 m 450

500

847m

The main
road at
Crianlarich
is only about
5km or 3m away!

ford

Lochan
Chailein

The upper
glen was home
to a herd of cows
when your author
surveyed Glen Lochay

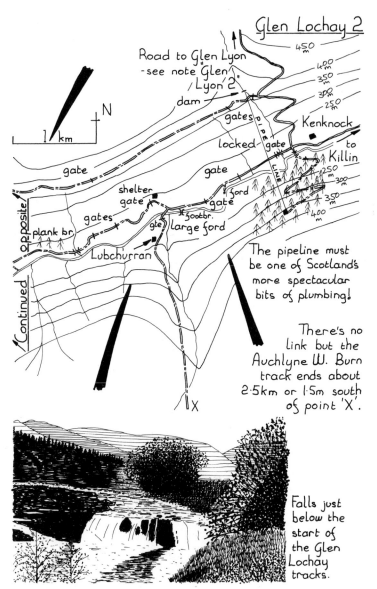

Glen Lochay 2

450 m
400 m
350 m
300 m
250 m

Road to Glen Lyon
- see note "Glen Lyon 2"

dam

gates

pipe line

Kenknock

locked gate

to Killin

gate

gate

gate

shelter gate

ford
gate

250 m
300 m
350 m
400 m

gate

gates

footbr.

large ford

plank br.

gte

gte

Lubchurran

Opposite

Continued

The pipeline must be one of Scotland's more spectacular bits of plumbing!

There's no link but the Auchlyne W. Burn track ends about 2·5km or 1·5m south of point 'X'.

X

Falls just below the start of the Glen Lochay tracks.

133

Auchlyne West Burn 1

The Auchlyne West Burn track runs along a wild moorland shelf above the Glen Dochart hamlet of Auchlyne
which is situated on a pleasant side road some 7 or
8 km south west of Killin. The track serves adits which
pick up water destined via the Glen Lochay pipe and
tunnels, for Loch an Daimh hydro-electric scheme.
The route is only 8km (5m) long but the initial 300m
climb ensures no lack of legwork - "Auchlyne Legs
Burn" would be a more appropriate name after
cycling up that hill!

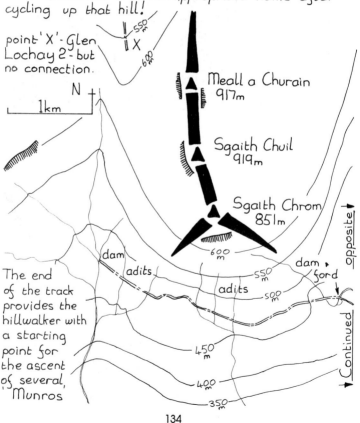

point 'X' - Glen
Lochay 2 - but
no connection.

N

1km

Meall a Churain
917m

Sgaith Chuil
919m

Sgaith Chrom
851m

dam
adits

dam
ford

adits

The end
of the track
provides the
hillwalker with
a starting
point for
the ascent
of several
Munros

opposite ▶

◀ Continued

134

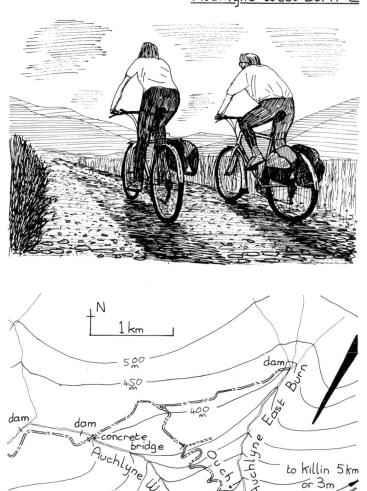

Drummond Hill 1

The forest tracks of Drummond Hill provide an almost endless combination of routes. Starting points are the car parks at either Mains of Taymouth or Rustic Lodge. Whilst walking (other than the short Forestry Commission marked routes) would prove somewhat tedious the tracks are ideal for mountainbiking, indeed this is encouraged by the Forestry Commission with yet more marked routes. At least two laps of the wood are needed to get one's bearings. The similarity of the contour tracks make it easy to get completely but harmlessly lost. Black Rock is the best viewpoint. There is no shelter but one is never very far from the start and there is no point in giving distances - just carry on until you drop!!

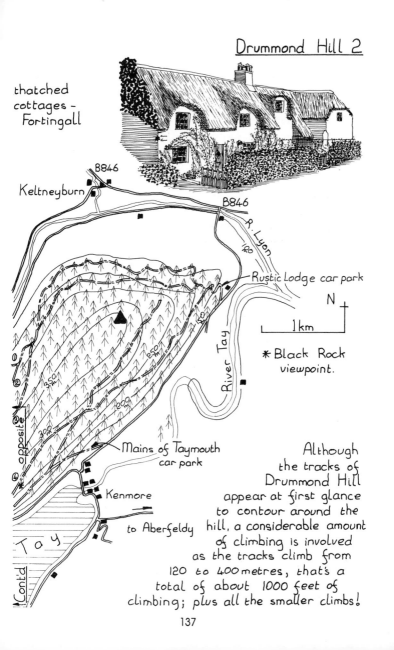

thatched
cottages -
Fortingall

B846

Keltneyburn

B846

R. Lyon
120

Rustic Lodge car park

N

1km

* Black Rock
viewpoint.

River Tay

250m
300m
350m
200

opposite

Mains of Taymouth
car park

Kenmore

to Aberfeldy

Tay

Cont'd

Although
the tracks of
Drummond Hill
appear at first glance
to contour around the
hill, a considerable amount
of climbing is involved
as the tracks climb from
120 to 400 metres, that's a
total of about 1000 feet of
climbing; plus all the smaller climbs!

Link Routes

The link routes shown demonstrate how long through routes are made up from the various page maps. Variations can be planned using further adjacent routes but these should provide a basis for extended exploration.

Fort William to Dalwhinnie

Link Route 1

Fort William to Dalwhinnie is a classic through route, 105km or 68miles in length with only 7km (4.5m) of metalled road at the Fort William end and only 5km (3m) of path (Luibeilt to Creaguaineach Lodge - refer Lairig Leacach 3+4). The rest of the route is on tracks. There are no roads to cross!! Allow at least two days by bike, four on foot. There is accommodation half way at Corrour and railway stations at each end of the route as well as Corrour.

138

Additional options for walkers are via Loch Ericht to Rannoch; via Culra and Ben Alder to Strath Ossian; and Glen Nevis as shown. Escape routes are available at Kinlochleven, via the Lairig Leacach; Corrour (by train or on foot to Rannoch); Moy and Kinloch Laggan so despite the road-free length of this route safe options do exist if weather conditions dictate.

Kinloch Laggan

Moy

Fersit

DALWHINNIE

River Pattack 2

Lochan na h-Earba 2

Lochan na h-Earba 3

Strath Ossian 2

Loch an na h-Earba 1

River Pattack 4

Loch Ericht 1

Note:- distances given below are approximate due to possible minor route variations.

Strath Ossian 4

walkers' route to S. Ossian via Ben Alder

Loch Ericht 2

Strath Ossian 6

walkers route to Rannoch via Loch Ericht

Continued opposite

Strath Ossian 5

X

Corrour

Rannoch

Continued below

450
400
350
300
250
200
150
100
50
0

R. Pattack

Loch Ericht

Dalwhinnie

85km 90km 95km 100km 105km

Continued above

400
350
250
200
150
100
50
0

Corrour

Loch Ossian

Jct to Fersit

Moy

L.nah-Earba

Ardverikie

Kinloch Laggan

45km 50km 55km 60km 65km 70km 75km 80km 85km

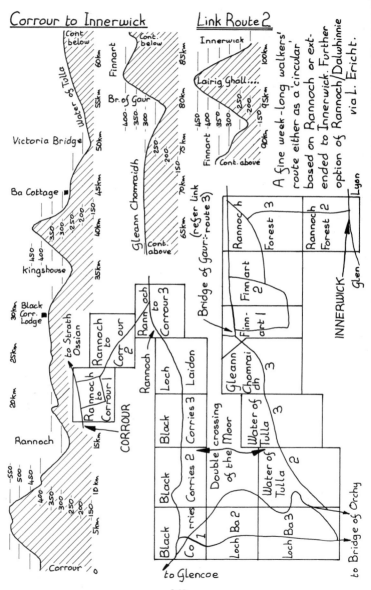

Corrour to Innerwick

Link Route 2

A fine week-long walkers' route either as a 'circular' based on Rannoch or extended to Innerwick. Further option of Rannoch/Dalwhinnie via L. Ericht.

Bridge of Gaur to Dalwhinnie
(and Kinloch Laggan)

Link Route 3

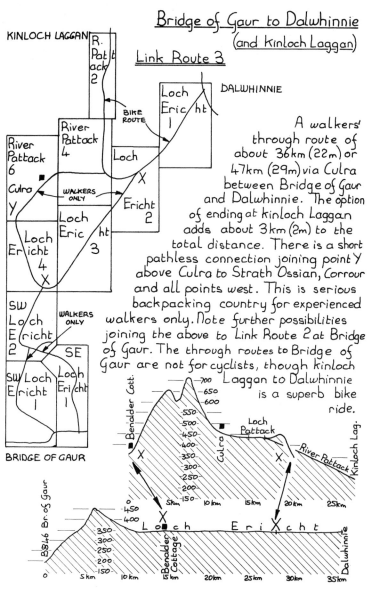

KINLOCH LAGGAN

R. Pattack 2

BIKE ROUTE

DALWHINNIE

Loch Ericht 1

River Pattack 4

River Pattack 6

Loch

Culra Y

WALKERS ONLY

Ericht 2

Loch Ericht 4 X

Loch Ericht 3

SW Loch Ericht 2

WALKERS ONLY

SE

SW Loch Ericht 1

Loch Ericht 1

BRIDGE OF GAUR

A walkers' through route of about 36km (22m) or 47km (29m) via Culra between Bridge of Gaur and Dalwhinnie. The option of ending at Kinloch Laggan adds about 3km (2m) to the total distance. There is a short pathless connection joining point Y above Culra to Strath Ossian, Corrour and all points west. This is serious backpacking country for experienced walkers only. Note further possibilities joining the above to Link Route 2 at Bridge of Gaur. The through routes to Bridge of Gaur are not for cyclists, though Kinloch Laggan to Dalwhinnie is a superb bike ride.

Benalder Cott.

700
650
600
550
500
450
400
350
300
250
200
150

X

Culra

Loch Pattack

X

River Pattack

Kinloch Lag.

5km   10 km   15km   20km   25km

B8846 Br. of Gaur

450
400
350
300
250
200
150

X   L o c h   E r i X c h t

Benalder Cottage

Dalwhinnie

0   5km   10km   15km   20km   25km   30km   35km

Loch Garry to Duinish

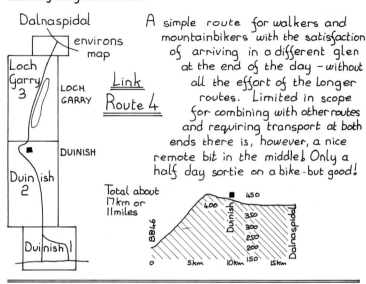

A simple route for walkers and mountainbikers with the satisfaction of arriving in a different glen at the end of the day – without all the effort of the longer routes. Limited in scope for combining with other routes and requiring transport at both ends there is, however, a nice remote bit in the middle! Only a half day sortie on a bike - but good!

Total about 17km or 11 miles

Auch Gleann to Glen Lyon

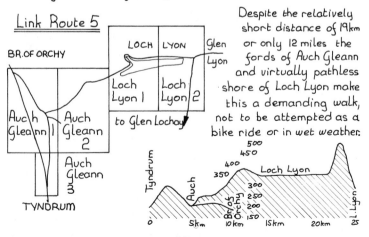

Despite the relatively short distance of 19km or only 12 miles the fords of Auch Gleann and virtually pathless shore of Loch Lyon make this a demanding walk, not to be attempted as a bike ride or in wet weather.

Book 3 complete! Researching and writing Book 3 has probably been the most satisfying yet, this being the second book where the research has been deliberate rather than haphazard. (Book 1, The Cairngorm Glens evolved rather than being researched and written with an end result in mind at the outset). The work now fits a pattern and reaching the objective, this page, is so much more satisfying as a result. I use the word "work" loosely as the thorough exploration of an area is a labour of love, only to be re-lived in the writing.

Rannoch is my type of country, long routes through remote areas, whether on foot or by bike is immaterial – it's being there that counts – boots or wheels are only a means to an end. Indeed, this book involved more walking than the first two resulting in walking some glens that could have been ridden – but what does it matter? It is the memories of the wild glens that count. Lying at night in Culra bothy in October listening to the stags bellowing outside; the beautiful combination of autumn colours and the first, fresh, snowfall of winter at Strath Ossian. One of the best memories was the traverse of the Grey Corries ridge from Meanach bothy by my wife and I; yes, we had a day off researching! (My wife incidentally accompanies me on all the research, types up notes and generally assists – without her help and company the task would be a lone campaign indeed – I digress!) Back on the Grey Corries ridge we were able to sunbathe at 1100 metres despite the lingering snow of late May. We saw two other people – a far cry from the backpackers' procession on the West Highland Way. I have avoided covering the W.H.W. as an entity because it has been the subject of other guides dedicated to it. The bits I cover are included because they fall into my arbitrary "glen" theme.

Work on Book 4 is now under way. Based around the Trossachs the terrain is in complete contrast to Rannoch, but the variety provides interest for you and I!